Decisions of Fate

—

COURSE AUTHOR
Rabbi Shmuel Super

COURSE EDITOR
Rabbi Mordechai Dinerman

COURSE CONSULTANT
Rabbi Edward Reichman, M.D.

CURRICULUM DEVELOPMENT
Rabbi Eli Raksin
Rabbi Yanky Raskin
Rabbi Naftali Silberberg

INSTRUCTORS ADVISORY BOARD
Rabbi Levi Dubov
Rabbi Yossi Mendelson
Rabbi Yochanan Posner
Mrs. Rivkah Slonim

Cover Art: *Quick Decisions*
Mirja Nuutinen, digital-on-paper collage of hand painting, photography, and drawing, 2023, Finland

Printed in the United States of America

832 Eastern Parkway, Brooklyn, NY 11213

718-221-6900
WWW.MYJLI.COM

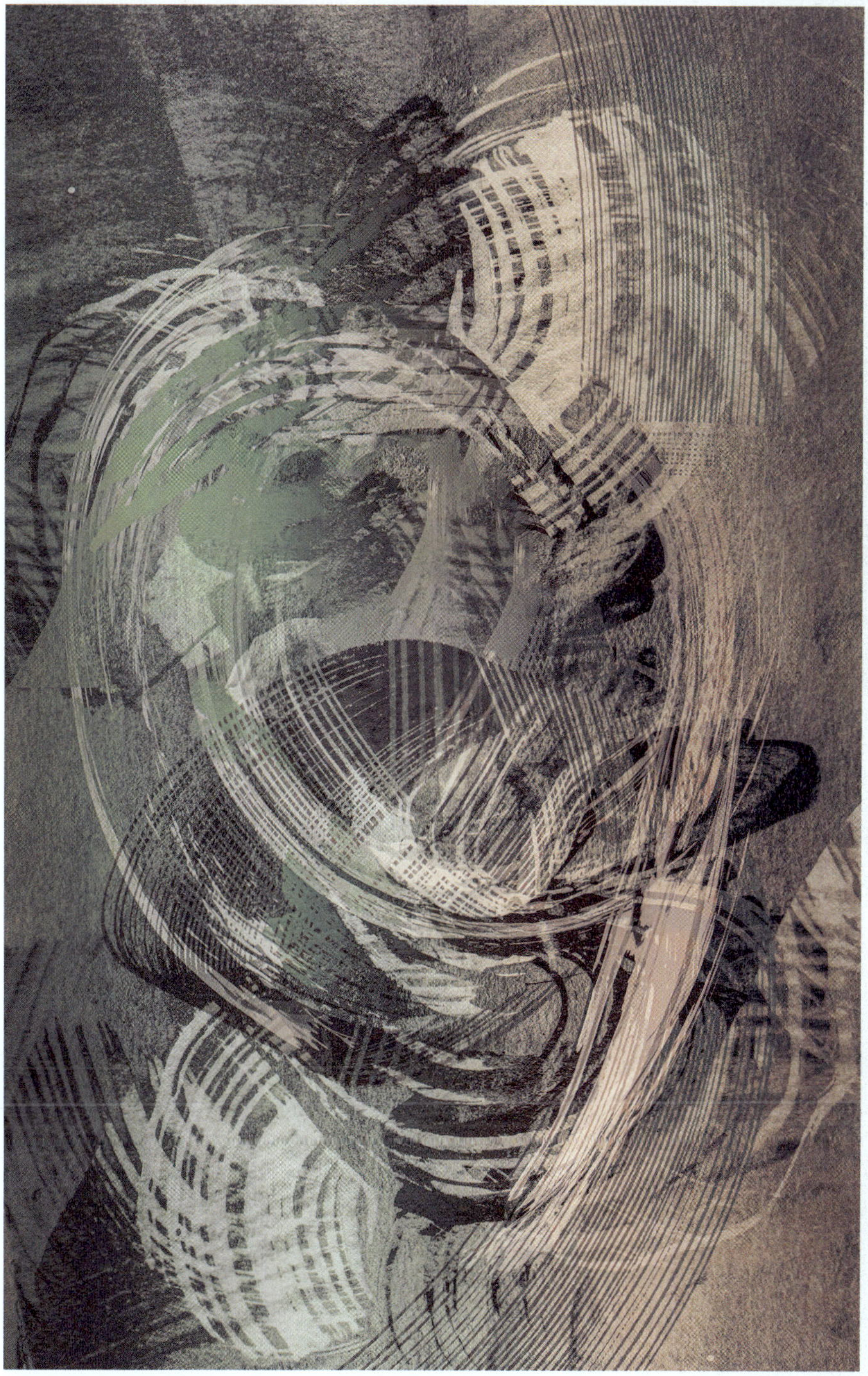

Decisions of Fate

Your Jewish Compass for Navigating Questions of Medical Ethics

COURSE TEXTBOOK

ADVISORY BOARD *of* GOVERNORS

Yaakov and Karen Cohen
Potomac, MD

Yitzchok and Julie Gniwisch
Montreal, QC

Barbara Hines
Aspen, CO

Ellen Marks
S. Diego, CA

David Mintz, OBM
Tenafly, NJ

George Rohr
New York, NY

Dr. Stephen F. Serbin
Columbia, SC

Leonard A. Wien, Jr.
Miami Beach, FL

PARTNERING FOUNDATIONS

Beinoni Foundation

David Samuel Rock Foundation

Diamond Foundation

Estate of Elliot James Belkin

Francine Gani Charitable Fund

Goldstein Family Foundation

Harvey L. Miller Supporting Foundation

Kohelet Foundation

Kosins Family Foundation

Leticia and Eduardo Azar Foundation

Lion Heritage Fund at Rose Foundation

Meromim Foundation

Myra Reinhard Family Foundation

Robbins Family Foundation

Ruderman Family Foundation

Schulich Foundation

William Davidson Foundation

Yehuda and Anne Neuberger Philanthropic Fund

Zalik Foundation

PRINCIPAL BENEFACTOR

George Rohr
New York, NY

PILLARS *of* JEWISH LITERACY

Shaya and Sarah Boymelgreen
Miami Beach, FL

Pablo and Sara Briman
Mexico City, Mexico

Zalman and Mimi Fellig
Miami Beach, FL

Edwin and Arlene Goldstein
Cincinnati, OH

Yosef and Chana Malka Gorowitz
Redondo Beach, CA

Shloimy and Mirele Greenwald
Brooklyn, NY

Dr. Vera Koch Groszmann
S. Paulo, Brazil

Carolyn Hessel
New York, NY

Edward and Inna Kholodenko
Toronto, ON

David and Debra Magerman
Gladwyne, PA

Yitzchak Mirilashvili
Herzliya, Israel

David and Harriet Moldau
Longwood, FL

Ben Nash
Sunny Isles Beach, FL

Eyal and Aviva Postelnik
Marietta, GA

Clive and Zoe Rock
Irvine, CA

Michael and Fiona Scharf
Palm Beach, FL

Lee and Patti Schear
Dayton, OH

Isadore and Roberta Schoen
Fairfax, VA

SPONSORS

Moshe and Rebecca Bolinsky
Long Beach, NY

Dr. Stephen and Bella Brenner
New York, NY

Rabbi Meyer and Leah Eichler
Brooklyn, NY

Steve and Esther Feder
Los Angeles, CA

Yoel Gabay
Brooklyn, NY

Dr. Gerald Gilbert Glass
Sunrise, FL

Shmuel and Sharone Goodman
Chicago, IL

Marc Kulick
New York, NY

Michael and Andrea Leven
Atlanta, GA

Joe and Shira Lipsey
Aspen, CO

Josef Michelashvili
Glendale, NY

Rachelle Nedow
El Paso, TX

Peter and Hazel Pflaum
Newport Beach, CA

Abraham Podolak
Princeton Junction, NJ

Dr. Ze'ev and Varda Rav-Noy
Los Angeles, CA

Zvi Ryzman
Los Angeles, CA

Larry Sifen
Virginia Beach, VA

Myrna Zisman
Cedarhurst, NY

Janice and Ivan Zuckerman
Coral Gables, FL

The Rohr Jewish Learning Institute gratefully acknowledges the pioneering and ongoing support of

George and Pamela Rohr

Since its inception, the Rohr JLI has been a beneficiary of the vision, generosity, care, and concern of the Rohr family.

In the merit of the tens of thousands of hours of Torah study by JLI students worldwide, may they be blessed with health, *Yiddishe nachas* from all their loved ones, and extraordinary success in all their endeavors.

DEDICATED IN LOVING MEMORY OF

Sala and Jack Tellerman

May the merit of the Torah study worldwide accompany their souls in the world of everlasting life and be a source of blessings to their family with much health, happiness, *nachas,* and success.

AND IN TRIBUTE TO

Abraham Podolak

With deep appreciation for his friendship and partnership with JLI and his commitment toward the furtherance of Jewish literacy, education, and continuity worldwide.

Citation Types

SCRIPTURE

The icon for Scripture is based on the images of a scroll and a spiral. The scroll is a literal reference; the spiral symbolizes Scripture's role as the singular source from which all subsequent Torah knowledge emanates.

SCRIPTURAL COMMENTARY

Throughout the ages, Jews have scrutinized the Torah's text, generating many commentaries.

TALMUD AND MIDRASH

The Talmud and Midrash record the teachings of the sages—fundamental links in the unbroken chain of the Torah's transmission going back to Mount Sinai.

TALMUDIC COMMENTARY

The layers of Talmudic teaching have been rigorously excavated in each era, resulting in a library of insightful commentaries.

JEWISH MYSTICISM

The mystics explore the inner, esoteric depths. The icon for mystical texts reflects the "*sefirot* tree" commonly present in kabbalistic charts.

JEWISH PHILOSOPHY

Jewish philosophic texts shed light on life's big questions and demonstrate the relevance of Jewish teachings even as the sands of societal values continuously shift.

JEWISH LAW AND CUSTOM

The guidance that emerges from Scripture and the Talmud finds practical expression in Jewish law, known as *Halachah* ("the way"), alongside customs adopted by Jewish communities through the generations.

CHASIDUT

Chasidism's advent in the eighteenth century brought major, encouraging changes to Jewish life and outlook. Its teachings are akin to refreshing, life-sustaining waters from a continuously flowing well of the profoundest insights.

LITURGY

The texts of the Jewish prayer book burst with the full spectrum of human emotion: from joy, to longing, to contrition, and to hope. They all share the authentic search for a meaningful encounter with G-d.

PERSPECTIVES

Personal, professional, and academic perspectives, expressed in essays, research papers, diaries, and other works, can often enhance appreciation for Torah ideas and the totality of the Jewish experience.

Contents

Foreword

Most of us have an overall desire to do what is right, and we can often intuitively identify an appropriate and ethical approach to fairly typical developments. Life, however, is far from straightforward, and we sometimes encounter scenarios that are multifaceted and ethically complex. Especially challenging are dilemmas involving health, medicine, and mortality. Faced with difficult choices, our moral confusion is exacerbated by the high stakes involved—life or death often hinges on a single decision.

If this has been true throughout history, it has been significantly amplified through the advent of modern medicine. Yesterday's science fiction is today's reality and standard. In terms of medicine and health, this is an incredible blessing. At the same time, it has invited a proliferation of ethical quandaries, the likes of which could hardly have been imagined until now.

When sudden circumstances cast us directly into the deep end of thorny moral quandaries, we may feel overwhelmed, lost, and unable to reach any decision with confidence. Even after conclusions have been reached, decisions made, and consequences delivered, we might remain plagued by guilt due to our internal uncertainty as to whether we made the right call.

To this end, the Rohr Jewish Learning Institute (JLI) is pleased to present *Decisions of Fate*. The four lessons of this course analyze ancient Torah principles and paradigms and apply them to the quandaries of today, demonstrating how the wisdom of our ancient tradition can provide sensitive guidance to help us reach difficult decisions with confidence and moral clarity.

Endorsements

Modern medical ethics relate to a huge range of issues that affects almost every person throughout the course of their life. Jewish medical ethics/halakhah addresses all these issues in depth. It offers solutions to complex and complicated medical ethical matters based on long-standing discussions, decision-making processes, and a tremendous number of sources. The series of lectures by the Rohr Jewish Learning Institute is an excellent opportunity to gain knowledge of the Jewish ethical perspective regarding modern medical issues.

RABBI PROFESSOR AVRAHAM STEINBERG, MD

Pediatric Neurologist and Director, Medical Ethics Unit, Shaare Zedek Medical Center, Jerusalem

Head, *Talmudic Encyclopedia*

Author, *Encyclopedia of Jewish Medical Ethics*

It is such a thrill to once again express excitement about the upcoming lectures by the Rohr Jewish Learning Institute. It is important in these times for every Jew to know that there are paths in medical ethics that are uniquely Jewish that may differ from the standard representations by the press of Christian approaches to abortion, assisted suicide, and human experimentation. Attending these lectures will be illuminating for many of us and provide practical advice for those facing some of the most difficult choices in life.

EDWARD R. BURNS, MD

Executive Dean and Professor of Medicine and Oncology
Albert Einstein College of Medicine

By looking at the ethical challenges of modern medicine through the lens of cases extracted from traditional Jewish law, this course provides a thoughtful, nuanced, and much-needed Jewish perspective on a wide range of controversial and morally challenging issues like abortion, termination of life-sustaining treatment, and many more.

ERIC A. FELDMAN, JD, PhD

Tri-Chair, Penn Faculty Senate

Deputy Dean for International Programs

Heimbold Professor of International Law

Professor of Medical Ethics and Health Policy
University of Pennsylvania Carey Law School

I congratulate the Rohr Jewish Learning Institute for embarking on this endeavor. It is so important that healthcare providers, physicians, nurses, ethicists, and others acquire the knowledge and skills to navigate the complexities of their patients' values and beliefs. This course offers a valuable opportunity to achieve this goal.

EZRA GABBAY, MD, MS, FACP, HEC-C

Associate Professor of Clinical Medicine

Associate Clinical Ethicist
Weill Cornell Medicine, Cornell University

Chairman, NYP-LMH Ethics Committee

This course has outstanding presenters and addresses topics of huge importance. It should prove of great interest to Jews and non-Jews alike.

ARTHUR L. CAPLAN, MD

Mitty Professor of Bioethics

Founding Head of the Division of Medical Ethics, New York University Grossman School of Medicine

The leadership offered in this program by the Jewish Learning Institute is timely and elucidates important understandings from the Jewish tradition as we face major societal challenges around these issues. This is a great opportunity for all of us to ponder the richness found in the Jewish tradition, for better understanding the complexities we all face. With much gratitude for this work.

KEITH G. MEADOR, MD, THM, MPH

Director, Center for Biomedical Ethics and Society

Anne Geddes Stahlman Professor of Medical Ethics

Professor of Psychiatry and Behavioral Sciences,

Vanderbilt University Medical Center

Professor of Ethics and Society, Vanderbilt Divinity School

Director, Integrative Mental Health, VHA

JLI has consistently provided courses of the highest caliber. The latest addition to the medical curriculum, *Decisions of Fate*, addressing the latest cutting-edge issues in medical ethics from a Jewish perspective, is no exception. The course might also be aptly titled, *Decisions of Faith*. In a world where the pace of advances in medicine is proceeding at a dizzying pace, spawning a myriad of complex ethical dilemmas, JLI brings to bear the millennia of our rich Jewish tradition, allowing us to view these issues through the lens of Torah. The topics span the gamut of life, from its beginning (including the timely topic of abortion), to its end, and JLI has mastered the perfect balance of both contemporary and traditional sources. My professional recommendation (prescription) is to take a healthy dose of JLI for a 4-week "course" (with refills).

RABBI EDWARD I. REICHMAN, MD

Professor, Department of Emergency Medicine

Professor, Department of Epidemiology and Population Health

(Biomedical and Bioethics Research Training) Albert Einstein College of Medicine

Author, *Anatomy of Jewish Law*

The course clearly incorporates all the key themes of modern medicine and the ethical challenges that we face. The course will enable a greater understanding of how Jewish medical ethics can make a distinctive contribution to modern medicine. The course comes at a time where scientific advancements are producing increasing numbers of ethical dilemmas. There is a great need for people to think through these issues and be equipped to make choices. I am delighted that such a course has been developed and wish it every success.

JUNE JONES, PhD, MSC

Senior Lecturer in Professional Ethics and Law
Edge Hill University, Ormskirk, UK

This course will prove to be a valuable asset, both for beginners and more experienced practitioners in the field of clinical medical ethics. Taking the claims of the world's great religious traditions seriously is crucial to respectful patient-centered care. I look forward to seeing the benefits from this thoughtful series rippling throughout the profession for years to come.

JON TILBURT, MD

Professor of Medicine and Biomedical Ethics
Mayo Clinic

In 1955 the Rebbe wrote, "To declare that true science, whose sole purpose is to learn the truth, cannot be in contradiction with our Torah, which is the 'Torah of truth'—on the contrary, the deeper science delves, the more it corroborates the principles and particulars of our faith, the faith of Israel."

This course will enlighten the participants about a Torah-holistic approach to medicine as it focuses on the impact of our most important medical technologies in preventing and preserving our health, as presented within a moral and ethical framework. Medical ethics is often viewed as a complex discipline. However, the Torah's perspective provides deep practical and spiritual insights in making challenging decisions about our health. I highly recommend attending this important course.

JOHN D. LOIKE, PhD

Co-director, Master's Program in Bioethics at New York Medical Center

Adjunct Professor in Bioethics, Columbia University

Professor of Biology and Bioethics, Touro University

Whether one faces medical issues personally or only confronts them in the news, understanding the traditional Jewish approach to medical dilemmas that begin before birth and extend beyond death can be quite challenging. Modern technology has transformed previously straightforward questions into much more complex issues requiring decisions that were never present in the past.

Decisions of Fate: Your Jewish Compass for Navigating Questions of Medical Ethics, the new JLI flagship course, offers the opportunity to delve into many of these complex issues that touch on core values of Jewish belief and require careful thought. I highly recommend the new JLI course as an ideal venue to examine them.

DANIEL EISENBERG, MD

Assistant Professor of Diagnostic Imaging, Thomas Jefferson University School of Medicine

Author of the upcoming *Judaism and Medical Ethics: Exploring the Traditional Jewish Perspective on Contemporary Medical Issues*

Medical ethics—especially when it touches upon questions of life and death—forces us to examine our most deeply held values and beliefs. *Decisions of Fate,* the four-part series on Jewish medical ethics from The Rohr Jewish Learning Institute, is an excellent opportunity to think about the Jewish tradition's views on what we hold most dear. It can also prepare us to face some of our most difficult medical challenges.

RABBI IRA BEDZOW, PhD

Associate Professor, Emory University School of Medicine

Executive Director, Emory Purpose Project

Continuing Education Credits

FOR ATTORNEYS

The course

Decisions of Fate

has been approved in these states for the fulfillment of continuing legal education (CLE) requirements:

United States

Alabama
Arkansas
California
Colorado
Delaware
Florida
Georgia
Idaho
*Illinois**
Indiana
Iowa
Kansas
*Kentucky**
Louisiana
Minnesota
Missouri
*Montana**
Nevada
*New Jersey**
*New York**
*North Carolina**
Ohio
Oklahoma
Oregon
Pennsylvania
South Carolina
Tennessee
*Texas**
*Utah**
*Virginia**
Washington
*Wisconsin**

*Pending approval at the time this book went to print

Continuing Education Credits

FOR MEDICAL PRACTITIONERS

ACCREDITATION STATEMENT

This activity has been planned and implemented in accordance with the accreditation requirements and policies of the **Accreditation Council for Continuing Medical Education (ACCME)** through the joint providership of New York Medical College and the Rohr Jewish Learning Institute. New York Medical College is accredited by the ACCME to provide continuing medical education for physicians.

CREDITS DESIGNATION

New York Medical College designates this live activity for a maximum of ***6.0 AMA PRA Category I Credits™***. Physicians should claim only the credit commensurate with the extent of their participation in the activity.

AMERICAN DISABILITY ACT STATEMENT

New York Medical College fully complies with the legal requirements of the Americans with Disabilities Act. If you require special assistance, please submit your request in writing thirty (30) days in advance of the activity, to continuingeducation@myjli.com

CONFLICT OF INTEREST DISCLOSURE POLICY

The "**Conflict of Interest Disclosure Policy**" of New York Medical College requires that faculty participating in any CME activity disclose to the audience any relationship(s) with a pharmaceutical product or device company. Any presenter, whose disclosed relationships prove to create a conflict of interest with regard to their contribution to the activity, will not be permitted to present.

New York Medical College also requires that faculty participating in any CME activity disclose to the audience when discussing any unlabeled or investigational use of any commercial product or device not yet approved for use in the United States. New York Medical College and ACCME staff have no conflicts of interest with commercial interests related directly or indirectly to this educational activity.

DISCLOSURE OF COMMERCIAL SUPPORT AND THE UNLABELED USE OF A COMMERCIAL PRODUCT

No member of the planning committee and no member of the faculty for this event has a financial interest or other relationship with any commercial product.

The members of the Planning Committee are:

Edward I. Reichman, M.D.—Reviewer
Professor of Emergency Medicine and Epidemiology and Population Health,
Albert Einstein College of Medicine

Disclosure: Dr. Reichman presents no relevant conflict of interest.

Mindy Wallach—Course Administrator
The Rohr Jewish Learning Institute

Disclosure: Mrs. Wallach presents no relevant conflict of interest.

To claim credit for attending the course (6 credits), professionals should request credit and submit their name, profession, email, and mailing address to their instructor or online at: **myJLI.com/continuingeducation** at the beginning of the course.

Instructions on how to complete course evaluations and download your certificate will follow by email.

LESSON

1

EXPERIMENTAL TREATMENTS

When emerging treatments offer hope of recovery, when is the risk justified? Discover the Jewish ethics of risking your life in the hope of extending your long-term prospects.

M'KOR CHAIM
Rebecca Schisler, oil on canvas, 2014, Connecticut

I. INTRODUCTION

Welcome to *Decisions of Fate*, a four-part course that will explore uniquely Jewish perspectives on areas of medical ethics with broad relevance to the general public.

The first of these studies examines Judaism's general approach toward health and healing. It then investigates how these principles can guide us through difficult dilemmas regarding the degree of risk we may or may not accept in pursuit of healing.

CASE STUDY

Vibhav Rangarajan, "The 'Cruel Joke' of Compassionate Use and Right to Try: Pharma Companies Don't Have to Comply," *Stat News*, June 2018

Radha's birth went perfectly. She was a healthy baby and met all of her developmental milestones—until it came to walking. My wife, Sonal, a pediatric gastroenterologist, recognized this and we had Radha evaluated by several specialists. None thought anything was physically wrong and indicated that she would learn to walk with the help of some physical therapy sessions.

They initially helped. Then Radha's progress slowed. Just after her second birthday, additional testing, including an MRI of her brain and spine followed by a genetic analysis, revealed that our daughter had metachromatic leukodystrophy. . . .

Children with the most severe form of metachromatic leukodystrophy develop symptoms like trouble walking or poor muscle tone before the age of 30 months. Once symptoms appear, the prognosis is grim. Radha's health will decline rapidly over the next three to six months. She will soon lose her ability to move, speak, see, and eat, and will be prone to seizures. The disease will then plateau for several years, leaving her in a vegetative state and unable to communicate. Our only hope is that she'll always understand us when we tell her we love her, but we may never know. Most children with metachromatic leukodystrophy don't survive beyond their 8th birthday.

Because we live in an era of rapid genomic innovation, gene-editing technologies such as CRISPR, proteomics, and rational drug design, I assumed that a disease caused by a single-enzyme deficiency was treatable. In my search for ways to help my daughter, I came across enzyme replacement therapies being developed for a number of conditions, including metachromatic leukodystrophy.

Shire Pharmaceuticals has developed a therapy for the disease and has even found a way to deliver it across the blood-brain barrier, which is no mean feat. The company has even completed a multicenter Phase 1/2 trial of the drug, called SHP-611 (also known as HGT-1110) in Europe, with what appear to be promising results. There was enough of a signal of therapeutic benefit from this trial to move forward with another one, though it appears to be several months to a year away.

Children with metachromatic leukodystrophy who were involved in the original trial have access to the drug as part of an extension of the trial. Radha developed the disease too late to take part in the first trial, and too soon to join the second one (if and when it happens).

Even so, that discovery gave me hope. It meant that Radha should qualify for what the Food and Drug Administration calls its expanded access program, also known as compassionate use. It governs the use of an investigational medicine that has not been approved by the FDA outside of a clinical trial.

Here's how it is supposed to work. A physician caring for a patient with a terminal illness who has exhausted all other treatment options and isn't eligible for a clinical trial appeals to the pharmaceutical company to provide an investigational drug that has undergone at least a Phase 1 trial, which studies the safety of a drug. If the pharmaceutical company agrees, the treating physician applies to the FDA for approval for expanded access to the investigational drug.

Thanks to policy changes at the FDA, it has become easier than ever for physicians to seek access to investigational drugs. The application form has been significantly simplified and now only one member of a facility's

Should we consult rabbis on medical treatment? **Mrs. Rivkah Slonim** responds: **myjli.com/decisions**

institutional review board needs to sign off on the petition. The FDA approves more than 95 percent of such requests, and does so swiftly, usually in a matter of a few days.

Radha's physicians followed Shire's protocol for applying for compassionate use exactly as directed on the company's website. Within a day or two, their request was denied, without any legitimate medical reason given. . . .

All of our efforts to get answers from Shire have been repeatedly rebuffed with vague, unsatisfying responses, leaving me to wonder why the company is denying my daughter's only hope. In fact, Shire has refused to correspond with me directly, and has instructed me to direct questions to it via my daughter's treating physicians.

Large pharmaceutical companies are notoriously risk averse when it comes to expanding access to medications that are still in the testing phase. Many refuse to grant access to investigational drugs outside of clinical trials, and efforts to lobby them to release the medication as part of compassionate use are often rebuffed.

One fear they have is that an adverse event, like an injury or death—even if it is not directly due to the medication—will derail a company's ability to push a drug forward for FDA approval, something they argue would ultimately undermine efforts to develop drugs that can help other families.

In response to this fear, FDA Commissioner Scott Gottlieb unveiled an updated policy on reporting adverse events that occur during compassionate use. It now requires reporting "only if there is evidence to suggest a causal relationship between the drug and the adverse event." . . .

The push for a federal right-to-try process culminated this week with President Trump signing a new law in a ceremony surrounded by patients with life-threatening illnesses and their families. In theory, this law will let patients and physicians bypass the FDA and go directly to pharmaceutical companies for access to investigational therapies that have undergone early testing. But it doesn't require pharmaceutical companies to accede to these requests. . . .

Much of what we do in medicine is based on analyses of benefits and risks. Shire has produced a drug that in early testing demonstrated safety with enough benefit to push forward follow-up trials. In Radha's case, the potential benefits of SHP-611 clearly outweigh the risks, but only if we get the drug to her soon, before her condition deteriorates further.

Compassionate use and right-to-try are billed as ways to give hope to patients who have exhausted all other options. From Radha's perspective, they are nothing more than a cruel joke, dangling a potential lifesaving therapy just out of her reach.

EXERCISE 1.1

1. **Do you consider it appropriate for individuals suffering from life-threatening illnesses to be granted access to experimental drugs that have not yet been approved as safe and effective? If yes, under what conditions?**

2. **Are there circumstances under which you believe drug companies should be required to provide access?**

Can a doctor ever say no? Talmudic sage **Rabbi Adin Even-Israel Steinsaltz** offers insight: **myjli.com/decisions**

FOUR JEWISH DOCTORS FROM ADRIANOPLE, TURKEY
Unknown artist: German school, watercolor on paper, c. 1600 (private collection)

II. HEALTHY OBLIGATION

The primary dilemma raised by the above case of Radha Rangarajan is this: How far should we go in our attempt to find healing? What degree of risk is acceptable in the pursuit of this goal? In order to appreciate Judaism's response to this dilemma, it is necessary to first probe the roots, in Jewish tradition, of the imperative to heal and the obligation to avoid danger.

TEXT 1

Caution

Maimonides, *Mishneh Torah*, Laws of the Murderer and Guarding Life 11:4

כָּל מִכְשׁוֹל שֶׁיֵּשׁ בּוֹ סַכָּנַת נְפָשׁוֹת, מִצְוַת עֲשֵׂה לַהֲסִירוֹ וּלְהִשָּׁמֵר מִמֶּנּוּ וּלְהִזָּהֵר בַּדָּבָר יָפֶה יָפֶה, שֶׁנֶּאֱמַר: "הִשָּׁמֶר לְךָ וּשְׁמֹר נַפְשְׁךָ" (דְּבָרִים ד, ט).

It is a positive mitzvah to remove any obstacle that might pose a danger to life and to be extremely careful regarding these matters, as it is stated, "Be cautious and preserve your life" (DEUTERONOMY 4:9).

RABBI MOSHE BEN MAIMON (MAIMONIDES, RAMBAM) 1135–1204

Halachist, philosopher, author, and physician. Maimonides was born in Córdoba, Spain. After the conquest of Córdoba by the Almohads, he fled Spain and eventually settled in Cairo, Egypt. There, he became the leader of the Jewish community and served as court physician to the vizier of Egypt. He is most noted for authoring the *Mishneh Torah*, an encyclopedic arrangement of Jewish law; and for his philosophical work, *Guide for the Perplexed*. His rulings on Jewish law are integral to the formation of Halachic consensus.

TEXT 2A

The Cost of Injury

Exodus 21:18–19

וְכִי יְרִיבֻן אֲנָשִׁים, וְהִכָּה אִישׁ אֶת רֵעֵהוּ בְּאֶבֶן אוֹ בְאֶגְרֹף,
וְלֹא יָמוּת וְנָפַל לְמִשְׁכָּב. אִם יָקוּם וְהִתְהַלֵּךְ בַּחוּץ עַל
מִשְׁעַנְתּוֹ, וְנִקָּה הַמַּכֶּה. רַק שִׁבְתּוֹ יִתֵּן וְרַפֹּא יְרַפֵּא.

If men quarrel, and one strikes the other with a stone or a fist, and the victim does not die but is confined to bed: If the victim subsequently gets up and walks around outside on his staff, the assailant is cleared. He pays only for the victim's involuntary idleness, and must provide for his cure.

THE NEW JEWISH HOSPITAL, BUILT BY SALOMON HEINE, HAMBURG, GERMANY
J. Gray, Hand-colored engraving: ink on paper, 1841 (Leo Baeck Institute, Center for Jewish History, New York, N.Y.)

TEXT 2B

Permission to Heal

Talmud, Bava Kama 85a

דְּבֵי רַבִּי יִשְׁמָעֵאל אוֹמֵר: "וְרַפֹּא יְרַפֵּא", מִכָּאן שֶׁנִּתַּן רְשׁוּת לָרוֹפֵא לְרַפְּאוֹת.

The school of Rabbi Yishmael taught, "He must provide for his cure"—this informs us that physicians are granted permission to heal.

PHYSICIANS SENT TO THE POLISH KING SIGISMUND BY JOSEPH NASI, DUKE OF NAXOS, TO CURE THE QUEEN

Arthur Szyk (1894 [Lodz, Poland]–1951 [New Caanan, Conn., via France and U.K.]), ink and paint on paper, in a style Szyk sometimes emulated: that of medieval and Renaissance illuminated manuscripts, 1927 (The Jewish Museum, New York, N.Y.)

BABYLONIAN TALMUD

A literary work of monumental proportions that draws upon the legal, spiritual, intellectual, ethical, and historical traditions of Judaism. The 37 tractates of the Babylonian Talmud contain the teachings of the Jewish sages from the period after the destruction of the 2nd Temple through the 5th century CE. It has served as the primary vehicle for the transmission of the Oral Law and the education of Jews over the centuries; it is the entry point for all subsequent legal, ethical, and theological Jewish scholarship.

If G-d decided to make someone sick, what's the rationale for going to a human for healing? The **Rebbe** on the doctor's job to help, not give up hope: **myjli.com/decisions**

TEXT 2C

Even So, Heal

Rashi, ad loc.

וְלֹא אַמְרִינַן: רַחֲמָנָא מָחֵי וְאִיהוּ מָסֵי.

We do not argue, "G-d* has struck; will the physician then go and heal?"

RABBI SHLOMO YITZCHAKI (RASHI) 1040–1105

Most noted biblical and Talmudic commentator. Born in Troyes, France, Rashi studied in the famed *yeshivot* of Mainz and Worms. His commentaries on the Pentateuch and the Talmud, which focus on the straightforward meaning of the text, appear in virtually every edition of the Talmud and Bible.

THE HOUSE OF THE BODY
Illustration (artist unknown) for *Helek Rishon mi-Sefer Ha-'Olamot—The Book of Worlds, Part 1*, or *Maaseh Tuvyah*—Toviyah's Work/Deed (play on words; a "good deed" is a *maaseh tov*): a book on the sciences—particularly medicine—and theology by Toviyah (ben Moshe HaKohen) Kats; engraving, Venice, Italy, 1708. The body's anatomical organs are shown here as analogous to the parts of a house. (Heb 7459.800*, Houghton Library, Harvard University, Cambridge, Mass.)

*Throughout this book, "G-d" and "L-rd" are written with a hyphen instead of an "o" (both in our own translations and when quoting others). This is one way we accord reverence to the sacred Divine name. This also reminds us that, even as we seek G-d, He transcends any human effort to describe His reality.

The Importance of Health

The following collection of texts explores Judaism's perspective on the importance of maintaining physical health.

The Study of Health

Talmud, Shabbat 82a

Rav Huna asked his son Raba, "Why do you not go to study from Rav Chisda, whose teachings are highly incisive?"

Raba replied, "Why should I go to him? When I do, he sits me down and teaches me mundane matters unrelated to Torah! He told me: One who goes to the bathroom should avoid straining themselves too much, for the rectum is supported by three muscles, and we must be careful to avoid dislocating them, which would bring the person to danger."

Rav Huna replied, "He deals with matters crucial for human life, and you call them 'mundane matters'! If this is what he teaches, you should most certainly go to him!"

A Tear in the Soul

Rabbi Avraham the Malach, cited in *Hatamim* 7:28

I am recording the words that my father, the Magid of Mezeritch, told to me on the eighteenth of Kislev, 5533 [1772], the day before his passing: "And you, my Avraham . . . it is important not to neglect your body, because a small tear in the body becomes a large tear in the soul."

The Mitzvah of Self-Care

Midrash, *Vayikra Rabah* 34:3

It is stated, "A kind person performs goodness for their own soul" (Proverbs 11:17). This virtue was exemplified by Hillel the Elder. He was once walking with his students and then branched off in a separate direction. They asked him, "Master, where are you going?" He replied, "To perform a mitzvah."

"Which mitzvah is that?" they inquired.

"To bathe in the bathhouse," he replied.

"Is that truly a mitzvah?" they asked. "Yes," he explained. "It is similar to the statues of the emperors that have been erected in theatres and circuses—the individual appointed to care for them duly cleans and rinses them, and for this effort, he is rewarded with sustenance and even elevated to be considered one of the kingdom's nobles. Similarly, I was created in the image and likeness of G-d, as it is stated in the Torah, 'In the image of G-d He made the human' (Genesis 9:6). How much more so must I care for my body!"

Healthy Divine Service

Maimonides, *Mishneh Torah*,
Laws of Character 4:1

Maintaining a healthy and wholesome body is a key element of Divine service, for we cannot properly understand or know anything of the Creator while sick. Therefore, we must distance ourselves from things that harm the body, and we must proactively conduct ourselves in ways that strengthen it and promote its health.

The Spiritual Connection

The Rebbe, Rabbi Menachem Mendel Schneerson, *Igrot Kodesh*, vol. 17, p. 242

Our sages teach that the body's limbs and sinews correspond to the six hundred and thirteen *mitzvot*. It is understood that one whose physical health is lacking can benefit from enhancing the health of their soul. When the soul gains fresh spiritual enthusiasm, it also improves the health of the body and increases the chances of successful medical treatment.

Working with the Body

Rabbi Yisrael Baal Shem Tov,
cited in *Hayom Yom*, 28 Shevat

The Torah commands us, "When you see the donkey of your enemy lying hopelessly under its burden, will you refrain from helping? [No,] you must certainly assist, together with him."

The Baal Shem Tov revealed the verse's deeper significance:

"When you see the donkey (*chamor*)"—when you reflect deeply on your material side (*chomer*), namely, your corporeal body—you will see that it is "your enemy". For the body detests the soul's yearning for G-dliness and spirituality. You will also see that it is "lying hopelessly under its burden," for G-d charged the body with fulfilling the Torah and *mitzvot* to elevate it, but the body is lazy in keeping them.

You might tell yourself, "I will 'refrain from helping' my body to fulfill its mission. Instead [I will conquer this enemy]: I will break out of my materialism through harsh asceticism and self-denial."

But this is not the way to apprehend the light of the Torah. Instead, "You must certainly assist, together with him"—you need to work together with the body, and assist it in attaining spiritual refinement and elevation; certainly do not try to break it with asceticism and the like.

TEXT 3

Cultivating Life

Midrash Temurah, *Otzar Hamidrashim*, vol. 2, pp. 580–581

מַעֲשֶׂה בְּרַבִּי יִשְׁמָעֵאל וְרַבִּי עֲקִיבָא שֶׁהָיוּ מְהַלְּכִין
בְּחוּצוֹת יְרוּשָׁלַיִם, וְהָיָה עִמָּהֶם אָדָם אֶחָד.

פָּגַע בָּהֶם אָדָם חוֹלֶה, אָמַר לָהֶם:
רַבּוֹתַי! אִמְרוּ לִי בַּמֶּה אֶתְרַפֵּא?

אָמְרוּ לוֹ: עֲשֵׂה כָּךְ וְכָךְ עַד שֶׁתִּתְרַפֵּא.

אָמַר לָהֶם: וּמִי הִכָּה אוֹתִי?

אָמְרוּ לוֹ: הַקָּדוֹשׁ בָּרוּךְ הוּא.

אָמַר לָהֶם: וְאַתֶּם הִכְנַסְתֶּם עַצְמְכֶם בְּדָבָר שֶׁאֵינוֹ שֶׁלָּכֶם!
הוּא הִכָּה וְאַתֶּם מְרַפְּאִים, אֵינְכֶם עוֹבְרִים עַל רְצוֹנוֹ?

אָמְרוּ לוֹ: מָה מְלַאכְתֶּךָ?

אָמַר לָהֶם: עוֹבֵד אֲדָמָה אֲנִי, הֲרֵי הַמַּגָּל בְּיָדִי.

אָמְרוּ לוֹ: מִי בָּרָא אֶת הַכֶּרֶם?

אָמַר לָהֶם: הַקָּדוֹשׁ בָּרוּךְ הוּא.

אָמְרוּ לוֹ: וְאַתָּה מַכְנִיס עַצְמְךָ בְּדָבָר שֶׁאֵינוֹ שֶׁלְּךָ!
הוּא בָּרָא אוֹתוֹ, וְאַתָּה קוֹצֵץ פֵּרוֹתָיו מִמֶּנּוּ?

אָמַר לָהֶם: אֵין אַתֶּם רוֹאִים הַמַּגָּל בְּיָדִי? אִלוּלֵי אֲנִי יוֹצֵא
וְחוֹרְשׁוֹ וּמְכַסְחוֹ וּמְזַבְּלוֹ וּמְנַכְּשׁוֹ, לֹא תַּעֲלֶה מְאוּמָה!

אָמְרוּ לוֹ: שׁוֹטֶה שֶׁבָּעוֹלָם! מִיָּמֶיךָ לֹא שָׁמַעְתָּ מָה שֶׁכָּתוּב:
"אֱנוֹשׁ כֶּחָצִיר יָמָיו" (תְּהִלִּים קג, טו), כְּשֵׁם שֶׁהָעֵץ אִם

MIDRASH TEMURAH

Midrash Temurah is a small midrash, attributed to the *tanna'im* Rabbi Yishmael and Rabbi Akiva. It was first published by Rabbi Chaim Yosef David Azulai, who found it in manuscript form, and appended it to the second part of his *Shem Hagedolim*. This midrash is copied in its entirety in the *Sefer Hapardes* (attributed to Rashi's disciples) and also cited by Me'iri (as "*Midrash Temurot*").

אֵינוֹ מְנֻכֵּשׁ וּמְזֻבָּל וְנֶחֱרַשׁ אֵינוֹ עוֹלֶה, וְאִם עָלָה וְלֹא
שָׁתָה מַיִם וְלֹא נִזְבַּל אֵינוֹ חַי וְהוּא מֵת, כָּךְ הַגּוּף - הַזֶּבֶל
הוּא הַסַּם וּמִינֵי רְפוּאָה, וְאִישׁ אֲדָמָה הוּא הָרוֹפֵא.

When Rabbis Yishmael and Akiva, and one other individual, strolled the streets of Jerusalem, they met an ill man.

"Rabbis," he asked them, "tell me how I might be cured."

"Do such and such until you are cured," they replied.

"Who afflicted me?" he pressed.

"G-d," they responded.

"You have interfered in an area beyond your jurisdiction," the invalid retorted. "G-d afflicted me, and you advised me how to be cured. Are you not defying G-d's will?"

"What is your occupation?" the rabbis questioned him.

"I am a farmer," he replied. "This is my scythe in my hand!"

They pressed further, "Who created the vineyard?"

"G-d," came the reply.

"You interfere in an area beyond your jurisdiction!" they countered. "G-d created it, and you are cutting its fruits!"

"Do you not see the scythe in my hand?" he rejoined. "If I did not plow, trim, fertilize, and weed, nothing would grow!"

"Foolish man," returned the rabbis, "have you never heard the verse, 'As for the human, their days are like grass' (PSALMS 103:15)? Just as a tree will not sprout without the farmer weeding, fertilizing, and plowing—and after sprouting, it will not live without water and fertilizer, but will die—the same is true of the human body: drugs and medication are its fertilizer, and the doctor is the farmer."

Samuel ben Zwi Hirsch Dresnitz, illustration from *Birkat ha-Mazon–Grace after Meals*, ink on parchment, Nikolsburg (modern-day Czech Republic), 1725. Detail from a *bentsher*, a book of blessings used at meals. The page that includes this illustration, depicting a vineyard, with the heading *Berachah Acharonah*–After-Blessing, continues with the blessing said specifically after consuming wine or grapes. (Braginsky Collection)

TEXT 4

Thank G-d!

Maimonides, Pesachim 4:10

אִם רָעֵב אָדָם וּפָנָה אֶל הַלֶּחֶם וַאֲכָלוֹ, שֶׁמִּתְרַפֵּא
מֵאוֹתוֹ הַצַּעַר הַגָּדוֹל בְּלִי סָפֵק, הַאִם נֹאמַר שֶׁהֵסִיר
בִּטְחוֹנוֹ מֵה'? וְהוֹי שׁוֹטִים יֵאָמֵר לָהֶם, כִּי כְּמוֹ שֶׁאֲנִי
מוֹדֶה לַה' בְּעֵת הָאֹכֶל שֶׁהִמְצִיא לִי דָּבָר לְהָסִיר
רַעֲבוֹנִי וּלְהַחְיוֹתֵנִי וּלְקַיְּמֵנִי, כָּךְ נוֹדֶה לוֹ עַל שֶׁהִמְצִיא
רְפוּאָה הַמְרַפְּאָה אֶת מַחֲלָתִי כְּשֶׁאֶשְׁתַּמֵּשׁ בָּהּ.

If a person is hungry and eats food in order to relieve themselves from that great discomfort, would anyone suggest that they have abandoned their trust in G-d? Only fools would posit such a thing! Rather, just as I thank G-d when I eat—for providing me with something edible that removes my hunger and provides me with life and sustenance—it is similarly appropriate to thank Him for creating the treatment I can use to heal my illness.

Kabbalist **Rabbi Dovber Pinson** on attaining well-being through spiritual and physical balance: **myjli.com/decisions**

TEXT 5

Authority Limits

Rabbi Shneur Zalman of Liadi, *Shulchan Aruch HaRav, Choshen Mishpat, Hilchot Nizkei Guf Vanefesh* 4

אָסוּר לְהַכּוֹת אֶת חֲבֵרוֹ, אֲפִלּוּ הוּא נוֹתֵן לוֹ רְשׁוּת לְהַכּוֹתוֹ, כִּי אֵין לְאָדָם רְשׁוּת עַל גּוּפוֹ כְּלָל לְהַכּוֹתוֹ, וְלֹא לְבַיְּשׁוֹ וְלֹא לְצַעֲרוֹ בְּשׁוּם צַעַר.

It is forbidden to hit another person, even with their consent. For we have absolutely no authority over our bodies to permit that they be struck, denigrated, or pained in any way.

RABBI SHNEUR ZALMAN OF LIADI (ALTER REBBE) 1745–1812

Chasidic rebbe, Halachic authority, and founder of the Chabad movement. The Alter Rebbe was born in Liozna, Belarus, and was among the principal students of the Magid of Mezeritch. His numerous works include the *Tanya*, an early classic containing the fundamentals of Chabad Chasidism; and *Shulchan Aruch HaRav*, an expanded and reworked code of Jewish law.

KAYIN AND HEVEL — CAIN AND ABEL
S. Ilan Block, digital painting, 2023, New Jersey

Is cosmetic surgery permitted? World-renowned decisor of Jewish law **Rabbi Hershel Schachter** responds: **myjli.com/decisions**

III. TAKING THE GAMBLE

Having clarified Judaism's overall approach to medicine, including the Torah's directives to avoid risks to our lives and to seek healing for our illnesses, it is possible to attempt the application of this approach to the nuanced dilemma of risk-taking in pursuit of healing.

EXERCISE 1.2

Based on the Jewish approach to health and healing outlined above, do you consider it appropriate for individuals with life-threatening illnesses to turn to experimental drugs that have not yet been approved as safe and effective?

Yes **No**

Provide the rationale for your response:

Who shall live and who shall die, and who gets to decide? **Rabbi Shlomo Yaffe** discusses rationing medical care: **myjli.com/decisions**

FIGURE 1.1

CHAYEI OLAM	***CHAYEI SHAAH***
long-term life	short-term life

TEXT 6

Rescue on Shabbat

Maimonides, *Mishneh Torah*, Laws of Shabbat 2:18

מִי שֶׁנָּפְלָה עָלָיו מַפּוֹלֶת, סָפֵק הוּא שָׁם סָפֵק אֵינוֹ שָׁם - מְפַקְּחִין עָלָיו. מְצָאוּהוּ חַי, אַף עַל פִּי שֶׁנִּתְרוֹצֵץ וְאִי אֶפְשָׁר שֶׁיַּבְּרִיא - מְפַקְּחִין עָלָיו וּמוֹצִיאִין אוֹתוֹ לְחַיֵּי אוֹתָהּ שָׁעָה.

If a building collapses on Shabbat and we are unsure whether someone is buried beneath its rubble, we must clear [the rubble as a potential rescue attempt, although such activity is generally prohibited on Shabbat]. If we indeed discover a living person, even if they are crushed by debris to the extent of being mortally wounded, we nevertheless continue clearing the rubble off the victim to allow them to live a short while longer.

When Jewish and medical standards conflict, what do you do? Jewish medical ethicist **Rabbi Edward Reichman, M.D**. responds: **myjli.com/decisions**

TEXT 7A

A Grave Question

Rabbi Yaakov Reischer, *Shevut Yaakov* 3:75

מֵרוֹפֵא מֻמְחֶה עַל חוֹלֶה אֶחָד שֶׁחָלָה אֶת חָלְיוֹ שֶׁקָּרוֹב לָמוּת בּוֹ, וְכָל הָרוֹפְאִים אוֹמְדִין שֶׁוַּדַּאי יָמוּת תּוֹךְ יוֹם אוֹ יוֹמַיִם. אַךְ שֶׁאוֹמְדִין שֶׁיֵּשׁ עוֹד רְפוּאָה אַחַת שֶׁאֶפְשָׁר שֶׁיִּתְרַפֵּא מֵחָלְיוֹ, וְגַם אֶפְשָׁר לְהֵפֶךְ - שֶׁאִם יִקַּח רְפוּאָה זוֹ, אִם אֵינוֹ מַצְלִיחַ חָס וְשָׁלוֹם, יָמוּת מִיָּד תּוֹךְ שָׁעָה אוֹ שְׁתַּיִם, אִי מֻתָּר לַעֲשׂוֹת רְפוּאָה זוֹ . . .

תְּשׁוּבָה: הוֹאִיל שֶׁדִּין זֶה הוּא דִּינֵי נְפָשׁוֹת מַמָּשׁ, וְצָרִיךְ לִהְיוֹת מָתוּן מְאוֹד בִּשְׁאֵלָה כָּזוֹ מִשַּׁ"ס וּפוֹסְקִים בְּשֶׁבַע חֲקִירוֹת וּבְדִיקוֹת, כִּי כָּל הַמְאַבֵּד נֶפֶשׁ אַחַת מִיִּשְׂרָאֵל וְכוּ', וְכֵן לְהֵפֶךְ - הַמְקַיֵּם נֶפֶשׁ אַחַת כְּאִלּוּ קִיֵּם עוֹלָם מָלֵא.

I received an inquiry submitted by an expert doctor regarding a terminally ill patient: The unanimous medical prognosis is that the patient will die within the next couple of days. However, the physicians suggest that there is a medicine that might cure him but might cause him to die within a couple of hours of taking it. Is it permitted to administer the medicine? . . .

My response is that this is a matter of life and death, which therefore requires exceptionally careful consideration. It is necessary to thoroughly review the relevant passages in the Talmudic and Halachic codes, for "One who kills a single

RABBI YAAKOV BEN YOSEF REISCHER C. 1670–1733

Renowned rabbi, Halachic authority, and author. He served on rabbinical courts in Prague, Ansbach, Worms, and Metz. He was accepted by contemporary rabbis as the ultimate authority on Halachic issues, and problems were addressed to him from all over the Diaspora and Israel. His most famous works are *Chok Yaakov*, an exposition on the section of the Shulchan Aruch pertaining to the laws of Passover; and his responsa *Shevut Yaakov*.

individual is considered as having destroyed an entire world, and conversely, the act of saving a single individual is considered as having sustained an entire world" (MISHNAH, SANHEDRIN 4:5).

TEXT 7B

Initial Thoughts

Rabbi Yaakov Reischer, ibid.

וְלִכְאוֹרָה הָיָה נִרְאֶה דְשֵׁב וְאַל תַּעֲשֶׂה עָדִיף,
כִּי חַיְשִׁינַן לְחַיֵּי שָׁעָה, אֲפִלּוּ מִי שֶׁכְּבָר הוּא גוֹסֵס מַמָּשׁ.

Apparently, it would seem appropriate to apply the principle of *shev ve'al taaseh*—"it is preferable to let the situation sit where it is and make no proactive move"—out of concern for the preservation of *chayei shaah*. This consideration applies even in the case of *goses*, a dying patient in the final throes of life.

TEXT 8A

Pursuing Long-Term Hope

Talmud, Avodah Zarah 27b

אָמַר רַבִּי יוֹחָנָן: סָפֵק חַי סָפֵק מֵת,
אֵין מִתְרַפְּאִין מֵהֶן. וַדַּאי מֵת, מִתְרַפְּאִין מֵהֶן.

הָאִיכָּא חַיֵּי שָׁעָה?

לְחַיֵּי שָׁעָה לֹא חַיְשִׁינַן.

Rabbi Yochanan stated, "When it is doubtful whether an invalid will live or die [and the only physician available is a heathen whose animosity toward Jews leads us to suspect that he might deliberately kill the patient], we do not approach that physician for treatment. However, if we are certain that without treatment the patient will die, we may approach that physician for treatment."

[The Talmud asks:] Are we not placing the patient's *chayei shaah* in potential jeopardy?

[The Talmud responds:] In such a case, the concern for *chayei shaah* can be disregarded.

EXERCISE 1.3

Complete the chart to summarize the cases mentioned in Text 8a:

STATE OF THE PATIENT	NATURE OF THE DOCTOR	MAY THE PATIENT VISIT THE DOCTOR?

TEXT 8B

Long-Term Source

Talmud, Avodah Zarah 27b

וּמְנָא תֵּימְרָא דִלְחַיֵּי שָׁעָה לֹא חָיְשִׁינַן?

On what grounds are we permitted to waive the concern for *chayei shaah*?

The Siege of Samaria

The Talmud derives the permissibility for people to risk their lives in the hope of a long-term cure from a biblical story about the siege on Samaria, the capital of the Kingdom of Israel.

In this spread we present the biblical text regarding the siege, supplemented with commentary.

II KINGS 6:24–25

24 A while later, King Ben-Hadad of Aram mobilized his entire army, ascended to
Samaria, and besieged it. 25 There was a great famine in Samaria. (1) The siege went
on for so long that the head of a donkey sold for eighty silver shekels, and a quarter
of a *kav* of doves' dung sold for five silver shekels. (2)

COMMENTARY

(1) **RABBI MEIR LEIBUSH WISSER, *MALBIM*, AD LOC.**

Samaria struggled with seven years of devastating famine before the Aramean siege began. The calamity was further compounded as a result of the invasion's timing: Ben-Hadad attacked during the harvest season, occupied the villages and fields surrounding the city, and built siegeworks around the city, so that even the meager crops that did grow never reached the starving city.

(2) **RABBI DON YITZCHAK ABARBANEL, AD LOC.**

The starvation was so extreme that people resorted to eating nonkosher donkey flesh. This was permissible according to Jewish law, given the circumstances, based on the Torah's directive to "keep G-d's laws and live by them"—from which the sages deduce that we must "live by them, as opposed to dying because of them."

The siege prevented the population from collecting firewood from wooden areas outside the city. In desperation, they collected dove dung as fuel to cook their meager rations of raw edibles. Alternatively, the intensity of the hunger drove people to search for undigested wheat kernels in doves' dung.

II KINGS 7:3–6

3 **Four men [3] stricken with *tzaraat* lingered outside the city gates. [4] They told each**
other, "Why should we sit here until we die of starvation? 4 If we decide to enter the
city, we will die there due to the famine in the city. If we stay here, we will also die. So
let's go now and defect to the Aramean camp. If they spare us, we will [be provided
food and] remain alive. And if they kill us—we are going to die anyway!" [5] 5 They
got up at twilight to go to the Aramean camp. When they arrived at the edge of
the Aramean camp, they saw that no one was there. 6 G-d had made the Arameans
hear the sounds of approaching chariots and horses—a vast force—and they told

COMMENTARY

[3] II KINGS 5; TALMUD, SANHEDRIN 90A AND 107B

The Talmud discloses the identities of the four *tzaraat*-afflicted men. They were Gechazi—the Prophet Elisha's disgraced former right-hand man—along with his three sons. The story of Gechazi's banishment was related earlier, in chapter 5: When Elisha refused to accept payment for curing the Aramean General Naaman of *tzaraat*, Gechazi was determined to take advantage of the situation. Gechazi approached Naaman independently, claimed to represent Elisha, and solicited a generous payment for himself. Elisha subsequently learned of Gechazi's betrayal and disassociated himself entirely from Gechazi. As a consequence of the prophet's displeasure, Gechazi contracted the same *tzaraat* disease that had afflicted Naaman. The Talmud includes Gechazi on its short list of individuals whose evil caused them to lose their share in the World to Come.

[4] LEVITICUS 13:46; MISHNAH, KELIM 1:7

Why were *tzaraat*-sufferers banished from the besieged city? The Torah prohibits individuals afflicted with *tzaraat* from entering the Israelite camp. During the Jewish stay in the Sinai Desert, such an individual would "dwell alone outside the camp" until the *tzaraat* had passed. In the Land of Israel, the same rule prevented those with *tzaraat* from entering a walled city. Although these four men were banished from the besieged city, they chose to linger outside its gates in the desperate hope that the city's inhabitants might provide them with some food.

[5] DR. ABRAHAM S. ABRAHAM, M.D., *NISHMAT AVRAHAM*, VOL. 4, P. 240

The Talmud views the *tzaraat*-sufferers' decision to risk defection to the Arameans as proof that the Torah permits an individual to risk their immediate survival (*chayei shaah*) in exchange for a chance at securing long-term

II KINGS 7:6–9

each another, "Look! The king of Israel has hired the Hittite and Egyptian kings to
attack us!" 7 So they arose and fled in the twilight, abandoning their tents, horses,
and donkeys; they left the camp as is and fled for their lives. 8 The *tzaraat*-afflicted
men reached the edge of the camp, entered one of the tents, and ate and drank. They
then carried off silver, gold, and clothes, and went and hid them. They returned and
entered another tent, and again carried away and hid the loot. 9 Then they told each
other, "We are acting incorrectly: today is a day of good news, and we are remaining
silent! It would be a sin to wait until daylight [to inform the besieged city of their
miraculous salvation]. Let us go immediately and report this to the king's palace." [6]

COMMENTARY

life (*chayei olam*). However, the Talmud's use of this case is baffling: If the head of these men was the immoral Gechazi, how can we view his conduct as precedent regarding moral choices? Rabbi Shlomo Zalman Auerbach explains that the biblical narrative chose to record his choice of action for posterity without attaching any form of condemnation or reservation. Furthermore, the *tzaraat*-sufferers were the ones who merited discovering and announcing the miracle that had taken place. Consequently, this episode forms sound precedent from which we may derive laws.

[6] ***SHEVET MUSAR* 14**

Rabbi Eliyahu Hakohen Ha'Itamri, an eighteenth-century ethicist, considers Gechazi's looting of the Aramean camp a cautionary tale regarding the allure of greed. Gechazi had contracted *tzaraat* in the wake of his egregious display of greed (see note 3). Although he had been banished from society and had no foreseeable way to benefit from the booty, Gechazi's greed was stronger than his good sense. He rushed to hide caches of silver and gold, although it would never bring him any real benefit.

***TZIDKAT HATZADIK* 73:1**

Conversely, Rabbi Tzadok Hakohen of Lublin, a nineteenth-century Chasidic thinker, considers Gechazi's actions positively: G-d presented Gechazi with an opportunity to choose between mindless looting and demonstrating that he had overcome his negative trait. When he indeed stopped and declared, "It will be a sin for us if we wait. . . ."—choosing to inform the population of Samaria of their salvation rather than keeping all the loot for himself—he demonstrated that he had begun to rise above his past failure.

TEXT 9

Desperate Defection

II Kings 7:3–4

וְאַרְבָּעָה אֲנָשִׁים הָיוּ מְצֹרָעִים פֶּתַח הַשָּׁעַר, וַיֹּאמְרוּ אִישׁ אֶל רֵעֵהוּ, מָה אֲנַחְנוּ יֹשְׁבִים פֹּה עַד מָתְנוּ. אִם אָמַרְנוּ נָבוֹא הָעִיר וְהָרָעָב בָּעִיר וָמַתְנוּ שָׁם, וְאִם יָשַׁבְנוּ פֹה וָמָתְנוּ.

וְעַתָּה לְכוּ וְנִפְּלָה אֶל מַחֲנֵה אֲרָם, אִם יְחַיֻּנוּ נִחְיֶה, וְאִם יְמִיתֻנוּ וָמָתְנוּ.

Four men stricken with *tzaraat* lingered outside the city gates. They told each other, "Why should we sit here until we die of starvation? If we decide to enter the city, we will die there due to the famine in the city. If we stay here, we will also die.

"So now, let us go and defect to the Aramean camp. If they spare us, we will [be provided food and] remain alive. And if they kill us—we are going to die anyway!"

KINGS

Biblical book. Part of the "Prophets" section of the Hebrew Bible, the book of Kings relates the story of the Jewish people and their kings and prophets, from the end of the reign of King David until the Babylonian exile (837–423 BCE). Written by the prophet Jeremiah, Kings is originally one book, later divided into two parts.

QUESTION

In which way is this case similar to that of the potentially murderous physician?

TEXT 10

Seizing Hope

Rabbi Yaakov Reischer, *Shevut Yaakov* 3:75

בְּרַם, אִם אֶפְשָׁר שֶׁעַל יְדֵי רְפוּאָה זוֹ שֶׁנּוֹתֵן לוֹ יִתְרַפֵּא לְגַמְרֵי מֵחָלְיוֹ, וַדַּאי לֹא חַיְשִׁינַן לְחַיֵּי שָׁעָה. וּרְאָיָה בְּרוּרָה לְחִלּוּק זֶה מִסּוּגְיָא דְּשַׁ"ס . . . אִם כֵּן, גַּם כֵּן בְּנִדּוֹן זֶה - כֵּיוָן שֶׁוַּדַּאי יָמוּת, מַנִּיחִין הַוַּדַּאי וְתוֹפְסִין הַסָּפֵק אוּלַי יִתְרַפֵּא.

וּמִכָּל מָקוֹם, אֵין לַעֲשׂוֹת הָרוֹפֵא כִּפְשׁוּטוֹ כֵּן, רַק צָרִיךְ לִהְיוֹת מָתוּן מְאוֹד בַּדָּבָר, לְפַקֵּחַ עִם רוֹפְאִין מֻמְחִין שֶׁבָּעִיר עַל פִּי רֹב דֵּעוֹת . . . וְהַסְכָּמַת הֶחָכָם שֶׁבָּעִיר.

If the possibility exists for this treatment to completely cure the patient from his illness, we can certainly disregard the concern for *chayei shaah*. This approach has clear precedence in the aforementioned Talmudic case. . . . Consequently, in our case, since the patient will certainly die without intervention, we ignore the certainty [that he will survive on his own for a few more days] and seize the chance of fully healing him.

The above decision notwithstanding, a physician must not take this decision lightly. It is necessary for the physician to weigh the situation carefully, to consult with the other expert physicians in that city, and in case of divergent views, to abide by the consensus of the majority of experts . . . and to procure the agreement of the local Halachic authority.

Is medicine shaped by evolving social philosophies and ethics, or does it adhere to timeless values? Watch **Dr. Yaakov Brawer**, Professor Emeritus at McGill University's Faculty of Medicine, discuss this in *Where Medicine Differs:* **myjli.com/decisions**

IV. DEFINING THE PARAMETERS

According to the above principle in Jewish law, when faced with a choice between securing *chayei olam*, long-term life, and *chayei shaah*, short-term life, *chayei olam* takes precedence. However, in order to apply this principle to specific cases, it is necessary to arrive at more precise definitions of the parameters of *chayei shaah* and the degree of risk that can be tolerated in pursuit of *chayei olam*.

TEXT 11

Terminal Boundaries

Rabbi Avraham Yitzchak Hakohen Kook,
Mishpat Kohen 144:3

אֵין בְּיָדֵינוּ רְאָיוֹת לִקְצֹב בְּבֵרוּר כַּמָּה יֶאֱרַךְ הַזְּמַן לָצֵאת מִכְּלַל חַיֵּי שָׁעָה לְחַיֵּי עוֹלָם. וּמִסְתַּבְּרָא מִלְּתָא שֶׁכָּל שֶׁאָנוּ יוֹדְעִים שֶׁעַל יְדֵי סִבָּה זוֹ שֶׁל הַסַּכָּנָה שֶׁהֵחֵלָּה פְּעֻלָּתָהּ תָּבוֹא הַמִּיתָה, בֵּין אִם תַּקְדִּים וּבֵין אִם תְּאַחֵר - הַכֹּל בִּכְלַל חַיֵּי שָׁעָה.

The boundary marking the transition from *chayei shaah* to *chayei olam* is not clearly delineated. However, it is logical to assume that as long as we know that the illness is already terminal, regardless of how much time will pass until death arrives, it is considered *chayei shaah*.

RABBI AVRAHAM YITZCHAK HAKOHEN KOOK 1864–1935

Rabbi, author, and thinker. Born in Latvia, Rabbi Kook served as a rabbi in eastern European communities before immigrating to Israel in 1904 to serve as the rabbi of Jaffa. In 1917, he became the first Ashkenazic chief rabbi of pre-state Israel, and he was a leading figure in the religious Zionist movement. Rabbi Kook wrote many books on Jewish thought and law—including *Orot Hakodesh*—most of which were published posthumously.

TEXT 12

The Twelve-Month Principle

Rabbi Shlomo Kluger, cited by *Darchei Teshuvah, Yoreh De'ah* 195:6

לֹא נִתְפָּרֵשׁ כַּמָּה הוּא הַשִּׁעוּר שֶׁל חַיֵּי שָׁעָה. וְאֵין לוֹמַר דְּאִם סוֹפוֹ לָמוּת תּוֹךְ שָׁנָה אוֹ שְׁנָתַיִם נָמִי יְהֵא נֶחֱשָׁב חַיֵּי שָׁעָה. דְּאִם כֵּן אֵיךְ מַשְׁכַּחַת לָהּ חַיֵּי עוֹלָם, הֲרֵי סוֹף כָּל אָדָם לָמוּת, וּמָה לִי שָׁנָה אַחַת אוֹ שְׁתַּיִם אוֹ מֵאָה, סוֹף סוֹף לְעוֹלָם לֹא יִחְיֶה, וְאִם כֵּן יִהְיֶה נֶחֱשָׁב הַכֹּל חַיֵּי שָׁעָה?

וְדֹחַק לוֹמַר דְּדַוְקָא אִם יָמוּת מֵאוֹתוֹ חֹלִי נֶחֱשָׁב חַיֵּי שָׁעָה. אֲבָל אִם יָמוּת מֵחֹלִי אַחֵר לֹא נֶחֱשָׁב חַיֵּי שָׁעָה, דְּזֶה אֵינוֹ, דְּמָה לִי מֵחֹלִי זֶה אוֹ חֹלִי אַחֵר . . .

דְּמֵהָא דְּקַיְימָא לָן דִּטְרֵפָה אֵינָהּ חַיָּה י"ב חֹדֶשׁ, מוּכָח דְּכָל שֶׁאֵינוֹ יָכוֹל לִחְיוֹת מֵחֲמַת חֹלִי זֶה י"ב חֹדֶשׁ וְסוֹפוֹ לָמוּת מֵחֹלִי זֶה בְּתוֹךְ י"ב חֹדֶשׁ לֹא נֶחֱשַׁב חַיָּיו רַק חַיֵּי שָׁעָה, אֲבָל אִם עוֹמֵד לָמוּת רַק לְאַחַר י"ב חֹדֶשׁ לֹא נֶחֱשָׁב חַיֵּי שָׁעָה, רַק חַיֵּי עוֹלָם.

The definition of *chayei shaah* is not clearly spelled out in Jewish law. It is clear that a life expectancy of one to two years cannot be considered *chayei shaah* because if so, what is *chayei olam*? After all, everyone is mortal, and what difference is there between one year, two years, or one hundred years—seeing that no one lives forever? Are we to categorize all life as *chayei shaah*?

RABBI SHLOMO KLUGER 1783–1869

Born in Komarow, Poland; for a time he was a shopkeeper, but in 1820, he assumed the rabbinate of Brody, where he served for almost 50 years. During his lengthy career, Kluger wrote over 160 volumes on the Torah, including *Sefer Hachayim*, an explanatory commentary on the first section of the Shulchan Aruch, and *Sefer Stam*, concerning the laws of writing a Torah scroll. He wrote hundreds of responsa, some of which appear in *Ha'elef Lecha* "Shlomo." His writings covered various branches of rabbinical literature, as well as biblical and Talmudic exegesis. Among his students was the famed Rabbi Yosef Dov Soloveitchik, author of *Beit HaLevi* and dean of the yeshiva in Volozhin.

Nor does it appear correct to say that *chayei shaah* only refers to a situation in which the patient will die from the specific illness for which they presently seek a cure, and not from other ailments. What difference should it make what illness will cause the person's death? . . .

Rather, it would appear that just as a *terefah* is defined as an ill person or animal that will not live more than twelve months, similarly, anyone whose illness will prevent them from surviving for more than twelve months has entered the category of *chayei shaah*. Conversely, if the illness will cause death only after twelve months, the interval is not considered *chayei shaah*, but *chayei olam*.

***NIR PERMANENT SUB SOLE*—NOTHING IS ETERNAL UNDER THE SUN**
Alex Levin, oil on canvas, 2016, Tel Aviv

FIGURE 1.2

Defining *Chayei Shaah*

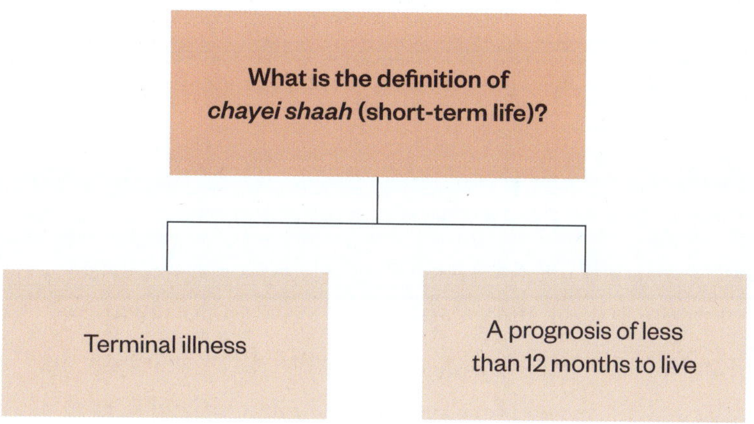

TEXT 13

Degrees of Danger

Rabbi Eliezer Yehudah Waldenberg, *Tzitz Eliezer*, vol. 10, 25:5

אוּלָם כָּל זֶה הוּא כְּשֶׁעַל כָּל פָּנִים הַסִּפּוּיִים לְחַיִּים אוֹ לְמָוֶת עַל יְדֵי בִּצּוּעַ נִתּוּחַ כָּזֶה שָׁוִים הֵם, אֲבָל לֹא בְּהֵיכָא שֶׁהַתּוֹצָאָה מֵהַנִּתּוּחַ הוּא שֶׁיָּמוּת עַל פִּי רֹב.

However, this permission to operate is valid only if the chances of life and death as a result of the surgery are equal—but not if, in the majority of cases, the patient will die as a result of the operation.

RABBI ELIEZER YEHUDAH WALDENBERG
1915–2006

Noted Halachic authority. Rabbi Waldenberg served as judge on the Supreme Rabbinical Court in Jerusalem and was known as an eminent authority on Jewish medical ethics and Jewish law. He published his Halachic responsa, *Tzitz Eliezer*, which is viewed as one of the great achievements of Halachic scholarship of the 20th century. He served as rabbi for the Shaare Zedek Medical Center in Jerusalem.

TEXT 14

For Any Hope

Rabbi Chaim Ozer Grodzinski, *Achi'ezer*, *Yoreh De'ah* 16:6

דְלְחַיֵּי שָׁעָה לֹא חָיְשִׁינַן הֵיכָא דְאֶפְשָׁר שֶׁיִּתְרַפֵּא,
אַף בְּאֹפֶן רָחוֹק, כָּל שֶׁנִּתְיָאֲשׁוּ מֵרְפוּאָתוֹ.

When faced with a case in which there is no alternative hope for a patient's survival, we disregard our concern for *chayei shaah* in exchange for even a remote possibility that the patient will be healed.

RABBI CHAIM OZER GRODZINSKI
1863–1940

Leader of Lithuanian Jewry in the years prior to the Holocaust. In his youth, he studied at the famed yeshiva in Volozhin and was known for his superb memory. In 1887, at the young age of 25, he was appointed judge of the famed rabbinical court of Vilna and was very active in the affairs of the community. He was one of the founders of the Agudath Israel movement and a pillar of the movement throughout his lifetime. His *Achi'ezer* is a collection of his responsa.

Illuminated page from a fifteenth-century copy of *The Canon of Medicine*, by Avicenna (also known as Ibn Sina). The influential medieval work was translated from Arabic to Hebrew in 1279 by Natan ha-Me'ati of Italy. (British Library, London)

TEXT 15

Experimenting with Hope

Rabbi Shlomo Zalman Auerbach, *Minchat Shlomo*, vol. 2, 82:12

מִי שֶׁחוֹלֶה בְּמַחֲלָה קָשָׁה אֲשֶׁר אֵין הָרוֹפֵא רוֹאֶה סִכּוּי לְהַצִּילוֹ בִּתְרוּפוֹת רְגִילוֹת, הֲרֵי זֶה דּוֹמֶה לְנִתּוּחַ, דְּאַף שֶׁיֵּשׁ סָפֵק שֶׁאִם לֹא יַצְלִיחַ יָמוּת מִיָּד, אֲפִלּוּ הָכִי מֻתָּר. וְהָכָא נַמִּי, גַּם כָּאן שַׁפִּיר רַשַּׁאי לְהִשְׁתַּמֵּשׁ בִּתְרוּפָה מְסֻפֶּקֶת.

The case of a seriously ill patient for whom the physicians see no hope of survival using standard drugs is similar to a case of a last-recourse surgery, which is permitted even though there is a risk that the patient will die immediately as a result. It is therefore permitted to use an unproven drug in this case.

RABBI SHLOMO ZALMAN AUERBACH 1910–1995

Halachic authority. Born in Jerusalem, Israel, Rabbi Auerbach served as the dean of Yeshivah Kol Torah. Recognized as one of the prominent Halachic authorities of the 20th century, he issued many important rulings related to the interface of Jewish law with medical ethics and modern technology. His rulings and responsa are collected in *Shulchan Shlomo* and *Minchat Shlomo*.

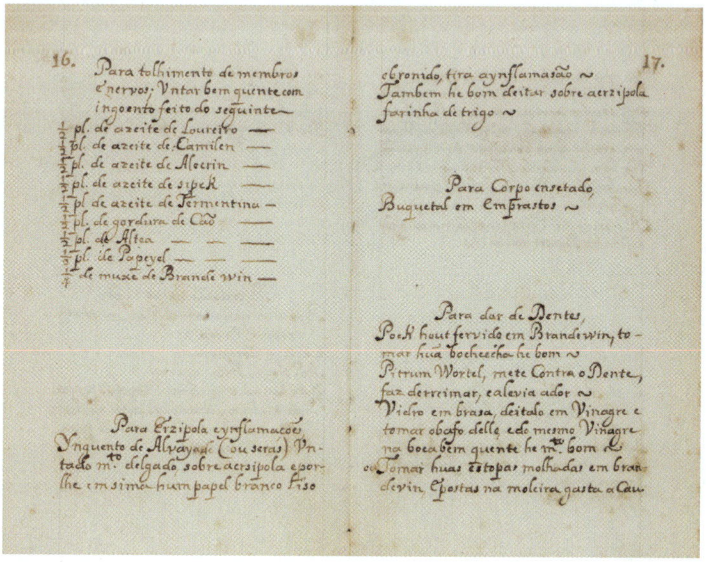

Handwritten pages from an unpublished medical book, a collection of remedies (*Catalogo de Diferentes Remedios para Diversas Sortes de Achaques, Achados por Experiencia Haverem Sido Bonos—Catalogue of Diverse Remedies for Various Ailments, Found by Experience to Have Been Good*), David Aboab, Amsterdam, 1685 (Ets Haim Library, Portuguese Synagogue of Amsterdam)

FIGURE 1.3

Risky Healing

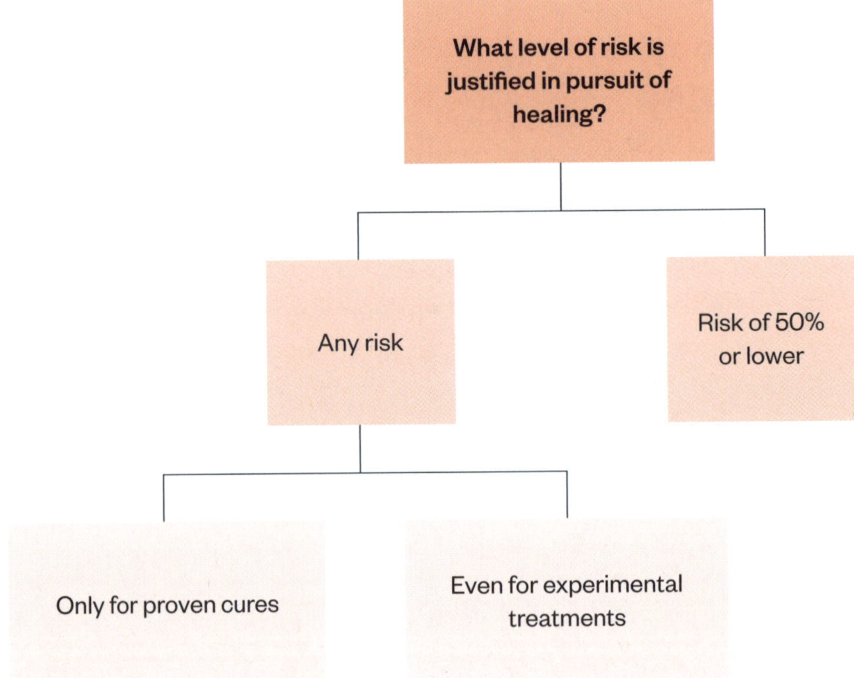

What is the Talmudic approach to risky medical procedures? Presentation by **Rabbi Mordechai Dinerman: myjli.com/decisions**

V. CONCLUSION

We now return to consider the questions raised by the case of Radha Rangarajan, based on the Jewish sources we have studied.

EXERCISE 1.4

1. **Do you consider it appropriate for individuals suffering from life-threatening illnesses to be granted access to experimental drugs that have not yet been approved as safe and effective? If yes, under what conditions?**

2. **Are there circumstances under which you believe drug companies should be required to provide access?**

The Rebbe's Advice on Health and Healing

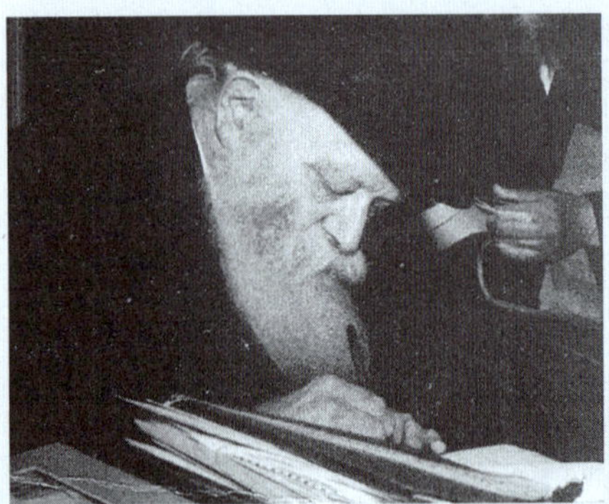

Over the latter part of the twentieth century, the Lubavitcher Rebbe, Rabbi Menachem Mendel Schneerson, corresponded with many thousands of individuals from all walks of life. His letters covered the full spectrum of Jewish scholarship and thought, and the human condition.

Presented here is a selection from the Rebbe's letters that address queries and concerns regarding health and healing.

Following Doctor's Orders

Surely I need not remind you that the Torah grants "the healer permission to heal," and it thereby supplies medicine with a degree of Torah authority. This negates the erroneous belief that G-d-fearing people need not strictly follow a doctor's instructions and may follow their independent perception. Instead, the opposite is true.

As is well known, Rabbi Shalom DovBer Schneersohn [the fifth Lubavitcher Rebbe] once pointed to his hand and told his son Rabbi Yosef Yitzchak, "See the preciousness of a Jewish body! For its sake, G-d poured forth the vastness of Torah and *mitzvot*." The Alter Rebbe similarly declared, "We have absolutely no idea how precious a Jew's body is to G-d!"

Igrot Kodesh, Vol. 10, p. 200

I was sorry to hear that you were not feeling too well, but I trust that by the time this letter reaches you, your health will have improved satisfactorily. Inasmuch as there is always room for improvement in all things, I wish you further improvement and complete recovery.

Not knowing what sort of a patient you are, I take the liberty of expressing my confident hope that you follow your doctors' instructions. Even if this may entail an enforced period of rest and interruption in your work, which no doubt you would be inclined to militate against, nevertheless, I am confident that you will overcome this, so as to expedite your complete recuperation.

The Letter & the Spirit
(Kehot, 1999), Vol. 3, p. 206

I was sorry to hear that you have not been in the best of health. I trust that you are carrying out the instructions of your doctor, especially as this is also a basic teaching of our Torah, as it is written, "heal you shall heal." (Exodus 21:19)

No doubt you also heard the saying of our Sages that the physical body of a person is G-d's property which was given to the person in trust to take care of. Thus, it is obvious with what care a person has to guard one's health and body, which is G-d's property.

English letter, dated Jan. 13, 1975

Trust in G-d

I trust you are firm in your trust in G-d, hence it is not necessary to worry about every detail. Leave these details to G-d, so that you can devote your attention to your business and to matters connected with Torah and Mitzvot. To follow a physician's instructions is one thing, but to worry about them is quite another and it has no place in one who trusts in G-d.

English letter, dated 1954

It is surely unnecessary to emphasize to you the importance of *bitachon*—complete trust in G-d—not just as an abstract belief, but in a way that truly permeates one's whole being.

For, in addition to this being one of the very fundamentals of our faith and way of life, it is also a channel to receive G-d's blessings, especially for the success of your medical treatment, which has to be undertaken in the natural order, inasmuch as our holy Torah itself gives authority and power to doctors to heal and cure.

English letter, dated November 17, 1972

You write that your wife's doctor instructed her to remain in the hospital for several days to undergo various tests, but that she is terrified of the hospital due to various (unfounded) concerns.

Please explain to her, in words she will appreciate given her present state of mind, that G-d created the world and that He directs it. . . . Nothing occurs here in this world without G-d, and whatever G-d wishes is done. At the same time, G-d wants us to provide Him with natural channels, so that He may carry out His will using natural means.

When . . . a person falls ill and seeks a doctor, the intention is not that the doctor will do whatever he wants, but rather, G-d has chosen this doctor as His agent, so that G-d may send healing through his agency. . . .

Consequently, when she is admitted to a hospital on her doctor's orders, she remains under G-d's protection. G-d will look out for her and ensure that all works out in the best way possible for the health of her body and her soul.

Igrot Kodesh, vol. 3, p. 441

Doctor's Limits

You wrote about a doctor's prognosis for your wife's health, and the impact this had on the two of you. This is surprising, for you seem to have forgotten the *Tzemach Tzedek's* dictum, "The Torah lends physicians permission to heal—specifically to heal and not to discourage people [with negative prognoses]."

This is more relevant than ever in the modern era, when fresh medical treatments and medications emerge daily. It is irrational to predict the future in the terms of which you wrote. I hope that you will be strong in your trust in the Creator, Who directs the specifics of our lives, and that in the near future, you will discover that this prognosis is false.

Igrot Kodesh, vol. 15, p. 187

While I am pleased to read in your letter a quotation about G-d being the Creator of the world Who also guides all its destinies, etc., this very good impression is weakened by the further tone of your letter, where you state that you want to be "realistic," based on the prognosis of physicians regarding your condition.

I want to tell you, first, that even from the realistic point of view, we must recognize the fact that very many times the greatest physicians have made mistakes in diagnosis. Moreover, in recent times we see that new discoveries are made daily in the medical field, with new "wonder" drugs and methods, which have revolutionized medical treatment.

Secondly, observing life in general, we see so many things that are strange and unbelievable, that to be truly realistic one cannot consider anything as impossible.

In a condition which is, to a large extent, bound up with the nervous system and the resistance of the organism, even medical opinion agrees that the stronger the patient's faith in cure, and the stronger his will to get better, the stronger becomes his ability to recover.

The Letter & the Spirit (Kehot, 1999), Vol. 3, p. 198

KEY POINTS

1 Jewish law considers preserving our health a religious obligation: we are commanded to avoid danger, and to seek healing when we are ill.

2 In Jewish thought, seeking medical treatment is fully compatible with faith in G-d. G-d created cures for illnesses and expects us to develop and utilize them, becoming His partners in sustaining human life. At the same time, we should remain cognizant that the efficacy of any treatment ultimately depends on G-d's will, and pray for His assistance.

3 Jewish law discusses two forms of life: short-term (*chayei shaah*) and long-term (*chayei olam*). Short-term life may be endangered in the pursuit of long-term life.

4 The definition of short-term life in Jewish law is subject to dispute: some authorities rule that any terminal illness qualifies, while others require a prognosis of less than twelve months to live.

5 There is also a range of opinions concerning the degree of risk to short-term life one is allowed to take in pursuit of long-term life. Some authorities maintain that only risks of 50 percent or less can be tolerated, while others maintain that any chance of success justifies any risk.

APPENDIX

TEXT 16

Defining Normal

Rabbi Moshe Feinstein, *Igrot Moshe*, *Yoreh De'ah* 3:36

וְחַיִּים הָרְגִילִים, הוּא שֶׁיִּהְיוּ חַיִּים בְּלֹא הַחֹלִי, שֶׁמִּצַּד הַטֶּבַע יָכוֹל לִחְיוֹת כְּחַיֵּי סְתָם אָדָם.

לֹא מִבָּעֵיא אִם יִתְרַפֵּא לְגַמְרֵי כְּבָרִיא מַמָּשׁ . . . אֶלָּא אֲפִלּוּ כְּפִי שֶׁיּוֹתֵר מָצוּי דְּאַחַר נִתּוּחַ הוּא נֶחֱלָשׁ, וְצָרִיךְ לִשְׁמִירַת הַרְבֵּה דְּבָרִים בַּאֲכִילָה וּשְׁתִיָּה וּלְמַעֵט בַּעֲבוֹדָה, וְהַרְבֵּה פְּעָמִים גַּם לִקַּח מִינֵי סַמִּים לִשְׁמֹר מַצָּבוֹ שֶׁלֹּא יֶחֱלֶה עוֹד הַפַּעַם, שֶׁגַּם כֵּן פָּשׁוּט שֶׁהוּא כְּחַיֵּי סְתָם אָדָם, שֶׁאִיכָּא בָּהֶם גַּם אֲנָשִׁים חֲלוּשִׁים שֶׁצְּרִיכִים לִשְׁמִירָה מִדְּבָרִים כָּאֵלּוּ, וְאֶפְשָׁר לָהֶם שֶׁיִּחְיוּ הַרְבֵּה שָׁנִים כַּאֲנָשִׁים הַבְּרִיאִים, וְגַם עוֹד יוֹתֵר. . .

אַךְ אִם הַנִּתּוּחַ יוֹעִיל, רַק שֶׁאֶפְשָׁר שֶׁיִּמָּשֵׁךְ בְּמַצָּב כָּזֶה זְמַן גָּדוֹל תַּחַת הַזְּמַן מוּעָט, וְיֵשׁ סָפֵק שֶׁהַנִּתּוּחַ יְמִיתֵהוּ תֶּכֶף, מִכֵּיוָן שֶׁאַף אִם יַעֲלֶה הַנִּתּוּחַ יָפֶה יִהְיֶה עָלוּל בְּכָל יוֹם מִצַּד הַמַּחֲלָה לָמוּת, אַף שֶׁיֵּעָשֶׂה אֶפְשָׁרִיּוּת לִמָּשֵׁךְ בְּמַצָּב סַכָּנָה כָּזֶה הַרְבֵּה זְמַן, מִסְתַּבֵּר לַעֲנִיּוּת דַּעְתִּי שֶׁאֵין לְהַתִּיר.

Ordinary life means life without that illness and a return to life's natural progression, according to which one is expected to live like the average person.

The above is needless to emphasize in the case that a patient is expected to gain total healing through

RABBI MOSHE FEINSTEIN 1895–1986

Leading Halachic authority of the 20th century. Rabbi Feinstein was appointed rabbi of Luban, Belarus, in 1921. He immigrated to the U.S. in 1937 and became the dean of Metivta Tiferet Yerushalayim in New York. Rabbi Feinstein's Halachic decisions have been published in a multivolume collection entitled *Igrot Moshe*.

the procedure. . . . However, it equally holds true in the more common scenario in which a patient is expected to remain weak post-surgery and will need to proceed with caution in several areas of life—such as maintaining a proper diet, avoiding excessive exertion, and, more often than not, taking medication regularly to prevent a relapse.

We must obviously consider the latter scenario to similarly be an ordinary way of living, for many individuals live naturally with weaknesses that require them to be cautious in the above matters—and it is possible for such individuals to live for many decades, with lifespans equal to those of healthy individuals and sometimes even longer. . . .

This is not the case, however, if the surgery is expected to enable a patient simply to continue in their ill state for a longer period—and it is coupled with a possibility that the surgery will result in instant death.

For, in such a scenario, a successful surgery nevertheless leaves the patient prone to die from this illness at any moment; it merely creates the possibility of surviving in a critical condition for a longer duration. It therefore appears, in my humble opinion, that such a surgery should not be permitted.

LESSON 2

EXTENDING LIFE

How does Judaism balance the desire to preserve life with concerns of reducing suffering? See how Jewish values inform a dignified approach to end-of-life care and advance medical directives.

UN ÁNGEL—AN ANGEL
Emma Cano, acrylic and pastel on cardboard, 2013, Cádiz, Spain

I. INTRODUCTION

Medical science and technology have made quantum strides. Several diseases have been virtually eradicated, effective remedies have been discovered for countless other diseases, and the average human lifespan has increased dramatically.

Greatly extended or *extendable* life spans are blessings that arrive with uninvited guests—fresh ethical and moral dilemmas regarding the end of life, such as: Should severely ill individuals have the right to actively end their lives? Should we seek to extend life as much as possible even for a patient with terrible suffering?

In this lesson, we explore the unique Jewish perspectives on these highly sensitive and equally complex dilemmas.

CASE STUDY A

Frances Mao, "David Goodall: Australian Scientist, 104, Ends Life 'Happy,'" BBC News, May 2018

> He perceived no other option, so 104-year-old scientist David Goodall left his home in Australia and flew across the world to end his life.
>
> The lauded ecologist and botanist did not suffer from a serious illness. But he wished to bring forward his death due to his diminishing independence.
>
> "My abilities have been in decline over the past year or two, my eyesight over the past six years," Dr. Goodall told reporters in Switzerland, where he had organised his death.

Medical ethics: Who can decide? Talmudic sage **Rabbi Adin Even-Israel Steinsaltz** shares insight: **myjli.com/decisions**

"I no longer want to continue life. I'm happy to have the chance tomorrow to end it."

Dr. Goodall travelled to a clinic in the city of Basel to voluntarily end his life. He said he resented having to leave Australia to do so.

The London-born academic had lived on his own in a small flat in Perth, Western Australia, until only a few weeks ago.

He stepped back from full-time employment in 1979, but remained heavily involved in his field of work.

In his last years, Dr. Goodall edited a 30-volume book series called *Ecosystems of the World* and was made a Member of the Order of Australia for his scientific work.

In 2016, aged 102, he won a battle to keep working on campus at Perth's Edith Cowan University, where he was an unpaid honorary research associate.

He made his final trip out of Australia last week with his friend, Carol O'Neill, a representative from assisted dying advocacy group, Exit International.

Mrs. O'Neill said the dispute in 2016 over Dr. Goodall's working space had affected him greatly. The row began when the university raised concerns about his safety, including his ability to commute.

Although Dr. Goodall ultimately prevailed, he was forced to work in a location closer to home. It came at a time when he was also forced to give up driving and performing in theatre, Mrs. O'Neill said.

"It was just the beginning of the end," she told the BBC.

"He didn't get to see the same colleagues and friends any more at the old office. He just didn't have the same spirit and he was packing up all his books. It was the beginning of not being happy any more."

Dr. Goodall's decision to end his life was hastened by a serious fall in his apartment last month. He was not found for two days. Later, doctors said he needed to engage 24-hour care or be moved into a nursing home.

"He's an independent man. He doesn't want people around him all the time, a stranger acting as a carer. He doesn't want that," Mrs. O'Neill said, prior to the scientist's death.

"He wants to have intelligent conversation and still be able to do the same things like catching the bus into town."

Switzerland has allowed assisted suicide since 1942. Other countries and jurisdictions have passed laws allowing people to voluntarily end their life, but many state terminal illness as a condition of eligibility.

The Australian Medical Association (AMA) remains strongly opposed to assisted dying, which it sees as an unethical practice of medicine.

"Doctors are not trained to kill people. It is deep within our ethics, deep within our training that that's not appropriate," president Dr. Michael Gannon said during last year's legislative debate in the state of Victoria.

"Now, not every doctor agrees with that," he added. Indeed, a survey of the AMA—Australia's most influential medical association—found four in 10 members supported right-to-die policies.

In his last days in Australia, the scientist revised his final letters and bade farewell to his extended family, including his many grandchildren.

An online petition raised $A20,000 (£11,000; $15,000) for the scientist to fly in business class to Europe. He rested with family in France before heading to Switzerland with his closest relatives.

His story gained attention locally at a time when his home state, Western Australia, is considering whether to debate assisted dying legislation.

The state government had publicly expressed sympathy for Dr. Goodall, but said any proposed legislation would cover only terminally ill patients.

Dr. Goodall said he would have preferred the chance to end his life in Australia. In his final appearances, he often wore a jumper emblazoned with the words "Ageing Disgracefully."

"I don't feel that anyone else's choice is involved. It's my own choice to end my life tomorrow and I look forward to that," Dr. Goodall said.

"At my age, and even at rather less than my age, one wants to be free to choose death, when the death is at the appropriate time," he told reporters.

"I certainly hope my story will increase the pressure for people to have a more liberal view on the subject."

SHABBAT VISIT
Lazar Krestin (1868 [Kovno, Lithuania]–1938 [Vienna, via Israel]), postcard, printed in the early 20th century, made from his 1894 painting, *Blessing of the Blind* (The National Library of Israel, Jerusalem)

EXERCISE 2.1

1. **Do you believe individuals like David Goodall should be free to choose to end their lives?**

2. **If not, consider this: Had Dr. Goodall been suffering from a terminal illness, would you believe he should be free to choose to end his life?**

CONTEMPLATION
Raquel Sanchez, oil on canvas, 2019, Israel

Jewish medical ethicist **Rabbi Edward Reichman, M.D.** discusses how Halachah addresses intervention for terminal prognoses: **myjli.com/decisions**

CASE STUDY B

A halachic query posed to Rabbi Eliezer Waldenberg, published in *Tzitz Eliezer* 18:62

An eleven-year-old boy has been suffering for the past two years from a cancerous growth in his brain stem. A significant accumulation of fluid was recently detected in his brain ventricles, and a ventriculoperitoneal shunt was surgically inserted to drain the excess fluid.

His physicians now seek to implant a different tube because the original tube has become blocked or infected. This procedure entails minimal risk, but it will prolong the boy's life and suffering. . . .

Is there an obligation to proceed with the surgery?

EXERCISE 2.2

How would you be inclined to respond to the dilemma posed by Case Study B?

FIGURE 2.1

Principles from *Cruzan v. Director, Missouri Department of Health*

1. A patient has a constitutional right to refuse medical treatment.

2. Artificial feeding is considered a medical treatment in this context, and the right to refuse treatment covers it as well.

3. The right to refuse treatment applies to both withholding care, as well as withdrawing it.

4. The right to refuse treatment pertains to all patients, even those who are not terminally ill.

Diploma earned by a Jewish physician from Pisa (Florence), Moses Crespino, from the University of Padua (Italy), in 1647. Several details distinguish this diploma's artful design from the equally artfully designed diplomas of non-Jews of the time: e.g., with the inclusion of a Hebrew passage from Psalms 111:10; and invoking "the eternal G-d" rather than the name of the Christian deity. (National Library of Israel, Jerusalem)

The Legal Status of Assisted Suicide

Jurisdictions where assisted suicide is legal

Jurisdictions where assisted suicide is illegal

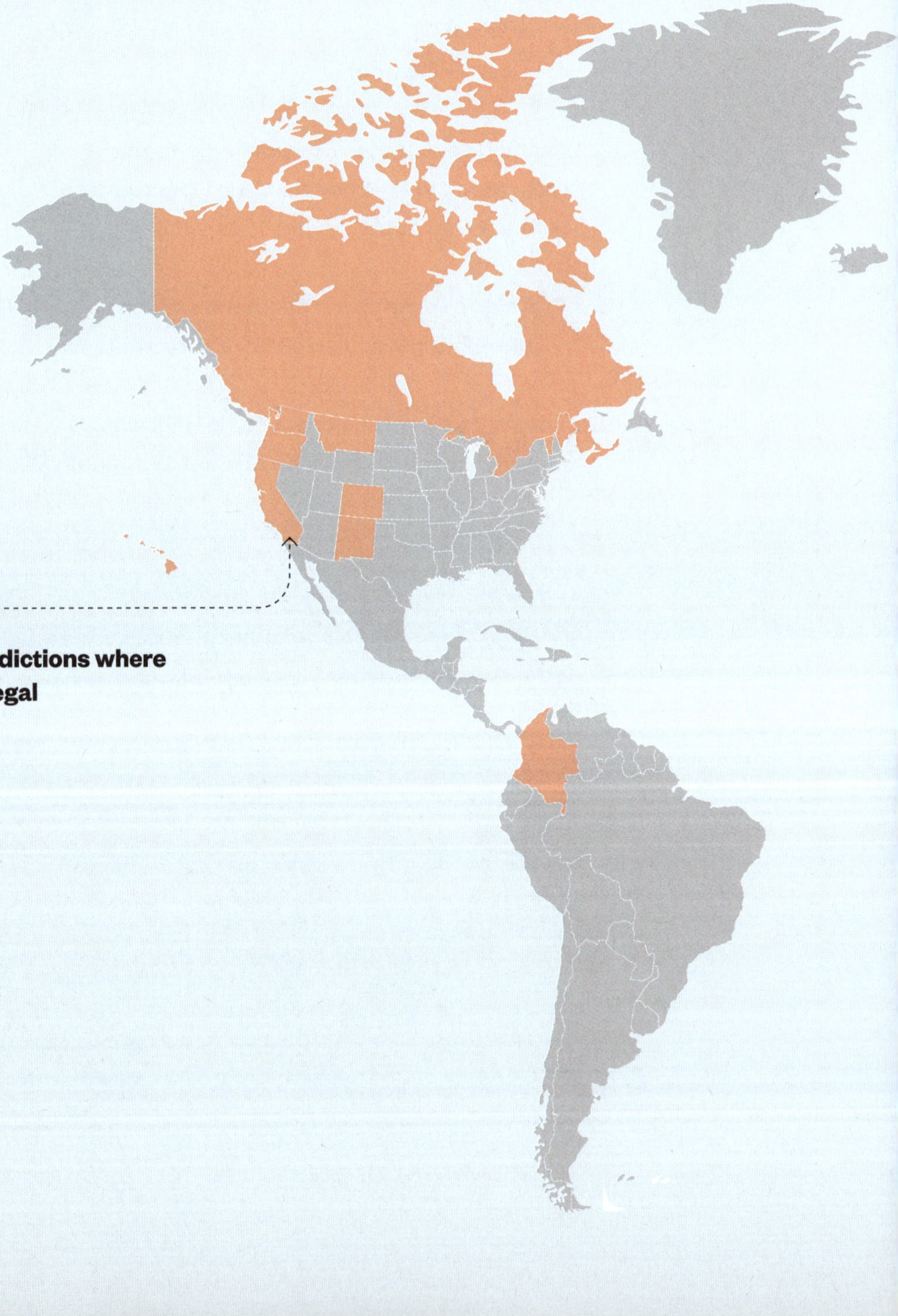

U.S. states and jurisdictions where assisted suicide is legal

California
Colorado
District of Columbia
Hawaii
Maine
Montana
New Jersey
New Mexico
Oregon
Vermont
Washington

The Meaning and Implications of the Divine Image

The Torah's Creation narrative states that the human was created "in the image of G-d." Later, the Torah refers to the human's Divine image as the reason for the severe prohibition of murder.

In this spread we present the biblical texts regarding the Divine image, supplemented with commentary explaining its meaning and implications.

GENESIS 1:26–28

26 **G-d said, "Let us make the human in our image, in our likeness.** 1 **They shall rule over the fish of the sea and the birds of the sky, over the animals and all of the earth, and over all the creatures that move along the ground."**
27 **And G-d created the human in His image; in the image of G-d He created the human; male and female He created them.** 2
28 **G-d blessed them and told them, "Be fruitful and multiply, fill the earth and subdue it. Rule over the fish of the sea and the birds of the sky and over all the beasts that tread upon the earth."** 3

COMMENTARY

1 RABBI OVADIAH SEFORNO, GENESIS 1:26

"In our image": This refers to humanity's intelligence that supports abstract thinking.

"In our likeness": This refers to the capacity for intelligent action. It informs us that the human ability to act with self-awareness and consciousness somewhat resembles the functioning of the angels.

The distinction is that the activity of the angels is performed involuntarily, whereas the human has a choice. In this respect, the human does not resemble the angels, but rather, G-d Himself, Who acts with absolute free choice.

2 MISHNAH, SANHEDRIN 4:5

G-d created the human species with a single individual—Adam. [G-d subsequently divided this being into a male and female, Adam and Eve.] This was done to teach us that G-d considers anyone who destroys a single life as if they have destroyed an entire world, and anyone who sustains a single life is considered as if they have sustained an entire world.

3 RABBI MOSHE BEN NACHMAN, GENESIS 1:28

G-d gave humans power and dominion over the earth. They have the ability to do as they wish with the animals and the creatures that move along the ground; they can build, uproot, mine copper from the hills, and so on. This is all included in the phrase, "Over . . . all of the earth."

GENESIS 9:5–6

5 I will demand an accounting for your lifeblood, [1] from every creature, and from
the hand of each human, from the hand of each person for that of their brother, [2] [3]
I will demand an accounting for a fellow human's life. 6 Whoever sheds human blood
will have their blood shed by humans, for G-d made the human in His image. [4]

COMMENTARY

[1] TALMUD, BAVA KAMA 91B

The verse states, "I will demand an accounting for your lifeblood." Rabbi Elazar reads this verse in an alternative form, as stating, "From your life I will demand an accounting for your blood," prohibiting suicide.

[2] RABBI YAAKOV TZVI MECKLENBURG, *HAKETAV VEHAKABBALAH*, GENESIS 9:6

There are two forms of murder. One is murder intended to be detrimental to the victim, as an act of revenge or in order to take the victim's money or the like. A second form of murder is to benefit the other, when someone is overwhelmed with tremendous pain and prefers death to life.

The Torah addresses both scenarios. Regarding murder with detrimental intent, G-d warns us, "from the hand of each human" By contrast, the second form of murder—committed with the consent of the suffering individual and for their benefit—may even be perpetrated by a virtuous friend, who may believe the act is a mitzvah! G-d therefore warns, "from the hand of each person for that of their brother."

[3] RABBI NAFTALI TZVI YEHUDAH BERLIN, *HAAMEK DAVAR*, GENESIS 9:5

The verse states, "From the hand of each person for that of their brother." With this choice of wording. G-d qualified that we are punished for murder in times of camaraderie and peace. However, at times of war and armed conflict, necessary killing in combat is allowed and does not incur punishment.

[4] *MECHILTA*, EXODUS 20:14

The Ten Commandments were engraved into two stone tablets: five on one tablet, and five on the other [so that each of the initial five appears parallel to one of the latter five].

"I am your G-d" appears on one tablet, and the corresponding line on the second tablet is, "Do not murder." The Torah thereby teaches us that one who spills human blood is considered to have reduced the Divine King's image.

This is analogous to a mortal monarch who gained dominion over a country. Statues of his image were duly erected, and coins were minted bearing his image. Sometime later, the people rebelled, and toppled the statues of the king and abolished his currency. By doing so they reduced the image of the king.

Similarly, whoever spills human blood is considered to have reduced the Divine King's image. Indeed, the Torah draws this very association and warns us, "Whoever sheds human blood will have their blood shed by humans—for G-d made the human in His image."

II. DIVINE DOMAIN

This lesson's exploration of the perspective of Jewish law on the above questions will first address physician-assisted suicide.

TEXT 1

The Divine Image

Genesis 9:5–6

וְאַךְ אֶת דִּמְכֶם לְנַפְשֹׁתֵיכֶם אֶדְרֹשׁ . . . וּמִיַּד הָאָדָם
מִיַּד אִישׁ אָחִיו, אֶדְרֹשׁ אֶת נֶפֶשׁ הָאָדָם.

שֹׁפֵךְ דַּם הָאָדָם בָּאָדָם דָּמוֹ יִשָּׁפֵךְ, כִּי
בְּצֶלֶם אֱלֹקִים עָשָׂה אֶת הָאָדָם.

I will demand an accounting for your lifeblood. . . . From the hand of each human, from the hand of each person for that of their brother, I will demand an accounting for a fellow human's life.

Whoever sheds human blood shall have their blood shed by humans, for G-d made the human in His image.

Rabbi Yitzchak Breitowitz provides the Jewish perspectives on assisted suicide and euthanasia: **myjli.com/decisions**

TEXT 2

Merciful Death

Rabbi Yaakov Tzvi Mecklenburg, *Haketav Vehakabbalah*, Genesis 9:6

נִרְאֶה לִי כִּי יֵשׁ שְׁנֵי אוֹפַנֵּי רְצִיחָה. אִם לְרָעַת הַנִּרְצָח - לִנְקוֹם נִקְמָתוֹ מִמֶּנּוּ, אוֹ לָקַחַת מָמוֹנוֹ וְכַדוֹמֶה; אִם לְטוֹבַת הַנִּרְצָח - כְּשֶׁהוּא מְשׁוּקָע בְּצַעַר גָּדוֹל וְיִבְחַר מָוֶת מֵחַיִּים . . .

עַל שְׁנֵי אֵלֶּה דִיבֶּר הַכָּתוּב, עַל הַהוֹרֵג לְרָעַת הַנִּרְצָח . . . יֹאמַר: "וּמִיַּד הָאָדָם" . . . וְאֶל הַשֵּׁנִי הַנַּעֲשֶׂה לִרְצוֹן הַנִּרְצָח וּלְטוֹבָתוֹ, אֲשֶׁר גַּם אִישׁ הַמְעוּלֶּה בְּמַדְרֵגָה וְגַם כְּשֶׁהוּא מֵאוֹהֲבֵי הַנִּרְצָח יְדַמֶּה כִּי מִצְוָה הוּא עוֹשֶׂה לַהֲמִיתוֹ כְּדֵי לְהַשְׁקִיטוֹ מִצַּעַר, עַל זֶה אָמַר: "מִיַּד אִישׁ אָחִיו".

There are two forms of murder: One is murder intended to be detrimental to the victim—as an act of revenge or in order to seize the victim's money or the like. A second form of murder is to benefit the other, when someone is overwhelmed with tremendous pain and prefers death to life. . . .

The Torah addresses both scenarios. Regarding murder with detrimental intent . . . the Torah warns, "From the hand of each human." . . . By contrast, the second form of murder—committed with the consent of the suffering individual and for their benefit—may even be perpetrated by a virtuous friend, who may believe the act is a mitzvah! The Torah therefore warns, "From the hand of each person for that of their brother."

RABBI YAAKOV TZVI MECKLENBURG
1785–1865

German rabbi and biblical exegete. Rabbi Yaakov served as rabbi in Königsberg, East Prussia. In 1839, he published *Haketav Vehakabbalah*, an important commentary that often demonstrates the indivisibility of the Written Torah and the Oral Torah.

TEXT 3

Until the End

Rabbi Yechiel Michel Epstein, *Aruch Hashulchan, Yoreh De'ah* 339:1

"הַגּוֹסֵס הֲרֵי הוּא כְּחַי לְכָל דְּבָרָיו" (שְׂמָחוֹת א, א) . . . וְאַף עַל פִּי שֶׁאָנוּ רוֹאִים שֶׁמִּצְטַעֵר הַרְבֵּה בְּגְסִיסָתוֹ וְטוֹב לוֹ הַמָּוֶת, מִכָּל מָקוֹם אָסוּר לָנוּ לַעֲשׂוֹת דָּבָר לְקָרֵב מִיתָתוֹ. וְהָעוֹלָם וּמְלוֹאוֹ שֶׁל הַקָּדוֹשׁ בָּרוּךְ הוּא, וְכָךְ רְצוֹנוֹ יִתְבָּרַךְ.

"A person in the throes of death is regarded as a living person in every respect" (*SEMACHOT* 1:1). . . . Though the patient is in terrible agony and they consider death preferable, we are nevertheless forbidden to do anything to hasten their death. The universe and all therein belongs to G-d, and this is His will.

RABBI YECHIEL MICHEL EPSTEIN
1829–1908

Noted author on Jewish law. Rabbi Epstein lived in czarist Russia and was chief rabbi of Novozybkov, a town near Minsk, and later, of Navahrudak, where he served until his death. A prolific writer, his primary work is *Aruch Hashulchan,* an expanded and reworked code of Jewish law.

QUESTION

Can you attribute any purpose or mission to the life of a terminally ill patient who is severely deprived of quality of life?

What should you say to someone who is begging to die?
Rabbi Manis Friedman:
myjli.com/decisions

TEXT 4

Good Deeds and Repentance

Mishnah, Avot 4:17

יָפָה שָׁעָה אַחַת בִּתְשׁוּבָה וּמַעֲשִׂים טוֹבִים בָּעוֹלָם
הַזֶּה, מִכָּל חַיֵּי הָעוֹלָם הַבָּא. וְיָפָה שָׁעָה אַחַת שֶׁל
קוֹרַת רוּחַ בָּעוֹלָם הַבָּא, מִכָּל חַיֵּי הָעוֹלָם הַזֶּה.

A single moment of repentance and good deeds in this world is greater than all the pleasures of the next world. And a single moment of bliss in the World to Come is greater than all the pleasures of the present world.

AVOT
(ETHICS OF THE FATHERS; PIRKEI AVOT)

A 6-chapter work on Jewish ethics that is studied widely by Jewish communities, especially during the summer. The first 5 chapters are from the Mishnah, tractate Avot. Avot differs from the rest of the Mishnah in that it does not focus on legal subjects; it is a collection of the sages' wisdom on topics related to character development, ethics, healthy living, piety, and the study of Torah.

FLAME KEEPERS
David Wander, U.S.A.

TEXT 5

The Brightest Light

The Rebbe, Rabbi Menachem Mendel Schneerson, *Likutei Sichot* 26, pp. 2–3

בִּשְׁעַת יֶעדֶער אִיד (יִהְיֶה מִי שֶׁיִּהְיֶה) וֶוערְט גֶעבָּארְן, וֶוערְט מִיט זַיין עֶצֶם לֵידָה אוֹיפְגֶעטָאן אַ נַייֶע הַמְשָׁכָה פוּן אֱלוֹקוּת אִין וֶועלְט, עֶס אִיז אַרָאפְּגֶעקוּמֶען (נָאך) אַ נְשָׁמָה וָואס אִיז "חֵלֶק אֱלֹקַה מִמַּעַל מַמָּשׁ" . . .

אִיז אָבֶּער בְּנוֹגֵעַ אִידְן בִּכְלַל, נִיט שַׁיָּךְ צוּ זָאגְן אַז שׁוֹין בִּשְׁעַת לֵדָתָם אִיז דָא אַן עִנְיָן פוּן אוֹר (וְגִלּוּי), וָוארוּם דִי נְשָׁמָה אִיז דָאך בְּהֶעְלֵם אִין גוּף, אוּן דֶער גִלּוּי פוּן אוֹר הַנְשָׁמָה אִיז תָּלוּי אִין בֵּרוּר וְזִכּוּךְ הַגוּף עַל יְדֵי הָעֲבוֹדָה – וָואס מֶער מֶען אֵיידְלְט אוֹיס דֶעם גוּף, אַלְץ מֶער אַנטְפְּלֶעקְט זִיך דִי נְשָׁמָה, אוּן עֶס לַייכְט דוּרְך אִיר גֶ-טְלֶעכְקַייט אִין דֶער וֶועלְט.

אוּן דֶערְפַּאר זָאגְט מֶען "טוֹב יוֹם הַמָּוֶת מִיּוֹם הִוָּלְדוֹ" (קֹהֶלֶת ז, א) וַוייל דִי כֹּחוֹת רוּחָנִיִּים וָואס אַ אִיד בַּאקוּמְט, זַיינֶען בְּיוֹם הִוָּלְדוֹ בְּלוֹיז בְּכֹחַ (אוּן אֵין אָדָם יוֹדֵעַ מָה מַּעֲשָׂיו). וֶוען קוּמֶען זֵיי לִידֵי גִלּוּי (וּשְׁלֵמוּת) – עֶרְשְׁט בְּיוֹם הַמָּוֶת.

At the time of birth, when a new soul—an actual part of G-d—descends, a fresh expression of G-dliness enters the world. . . .

At the actual moment of birth, the soul's light and revelation remain concealed within a corporeal

RABBI MENACHEM MENDEL SCHNEERSON 1902–1994

The towering Jewish leader of the 20th century, known as "the Lubavitcher Rebbe," or simply as "the Rebbe." Born in southern Ukraine, the Rebbe escaped Nazi-occupied Europe, arriving in the U.S. in June 1941. The Rebbe inspired and guided the revival of traditional Judaism after the European devastation, impacting virtually every Jewish community the world over. The Rebbe often emphasized that the performance of just one additional good deed could usher in the era of Mashiach. The Rebbe's scholarly talks and writings have been printed in more than 200 volumes.

body. Its expression depends on the person actively sublimating their body through Divine service. The more spiritual refinement a person introduces to their body, the brighter their soul shines forth, and the more it illuminates the world with G-dliness.

This insight explains the verse, "The day of death is better than the day of birth" (ECCLESIASTES 7:1). The spiritual powers we receive at birth exist only in a state of potential (and it is impossible to predict the extent of their eventual actualization). When do they radiate in their greatest brightness? At the end of life.

JACOB BLESSES HIS SONS ON HIS DEATHBED
Yoram Raanan, acrylic on canvas, 2013–2014

TEXT 6

Learning Meaning

Rabbi Yitzchak Breitowitz, "The Right to Die: A Halachic Approach," www.jlaw.com

The reader may legitimately ask: What use is the life of a person who is comatose and incapable of any cognitive brain functioning? What use is an anencephalic child? Keep in mind, however, that a Jew believes in a soul and that the body is simply a receptacle for the person's true spiritual essence. Souls come to earth for many, many purposes and we don't know why G-d sends souls into this life. Sometimes it could be that the spiritual destiny of a soul is to elicit certain responses on our part. The soul exists to teach us certain things about the meaning of life and love and how we relate to the dignity of a human being; and when we fail to respond with sensitivity and respect for the unconditional value of that person's life, we kill off a small part of ourselves as well.

RABBI YITZCHAK A. BREITOWITZ
1954–

Author, educator, and lecturer. Rabbi Breitowitz obtained his rabbinical ordination from Ner Israel Rabbinical College and his BA from Johns Hopkins University, and he graduated magna cum laude from Harvard Law School. In 1983, he joined the faculty of the University of Maryland School of Law, specializing in bankruptcy and commercial law. Rabbi Breitowitz currently lives in Jerusalem.

III. TO TREAT OR NOT TO TREAT

The above discussion focused on physician-assisted suicide and the removal of a patient from a ventilator, both of which are *active* steps. But what about *passively* withholding medical care? Does Jewish law instruct that terminally ill patients suffering respiratory arrest be placed on a ventilator in the first place? Must a patient under similar circumstances accept antibiotics to cure their pneumonia or endure another round of chemotherapy?

The following section explores a range of Jewish perspectives on withholding care.

EXERCISE 2.3

After each of the next two readings (Texts 7 and 8), please list the implications of the reading, in terms of the permissibility of withholding treatment from a terminally ill patient.

Is it OK to pray for someone's death if they are suffering? **Rabbi Yitzchak Schochet** responds: **myjli.com/decisions**

TEXT 7

Praying for Death

Talmud, Ketubot 104a

הַהוּא יוֹמָא דְנָח נַפְשֵׁיה דְרַבִּי, גָזְרוּ רַבָּנָן תַּעֲנִיתָא וּבָעוּ רַחֲמֵי . . . סְלִיקָא אַמְתֵיה דְרַבִּי לְאִיגְרָא. אָמְרָה: עֶלְיוֹנִים מְבַקְשִׁין אֶת רַבִּי, וְהַתַּחְתּוֹנִים מְבַקְשִׁין אֶת רַבִּי, יְהִי רָצוֹן שֶׁיָכוֹפוּ תַּחְתּוֹנִים אֶת הָעֶלְיוֹנִים.

כֵּיוָן דְחַזָאִי . . . וְקָמִצְטַעֵר, אָמְרָה: יְהִי רָצוֹן שֶׁיָכוֹפוּ עֶלְיוֹנִים אֶת הַתַּחְתּוֹנִים.

וְלָא הָווּ שַׁתְקֵי רַבָּנָן מִלְמִיבָּעֵי רַחֲמֵי. שָׁקְלָה כּוּזָא, שַׁדְיָא מֵאִיגְרָא לְאַרְעָא. אִשְׁתִּיקוּ מֵרַחֲמֵי, וְנָח נַפְשֵׁיה דְרַבִּי.

This is what occurred on the day that Rabbi Yehudah Hanasi died: The sages proclaimed a fast and they supplicated for Divine mercy [so that he would not depart from the world]. . . . Rabbi Yehudah's maid went up to the attic and prayed: "The angels on high ask for Rabbi Yehudah to ascend, and the people below ask for Rabbi Yehudah to remain. May it be Your will that those below prevail over those above."

Later, however, when she saw . . . that he was in great pain, she prayed, "May it be Your will that those above prevail over those below."

BABYLONIAN TALMUD

A literary work of monumental proportions that draws upon the legal, spiritual, intellectual, ethical, and historical traditions of Judaism. The 37 tractates of the Babylonian Talmud contain the teachings of the Jewish sages from the period after the destruction of the 2nd Temple through the 5th century CE. It has served as the primary vehicle for the transmission of the Oral Law and the education of Jews over the centuries; it is the entry point for all subsequent legal, ethical, and theological Jewish scholarship.

The sages, however, would not cease praying [which prevented the Heavens from gathering his soul]. So she grabbed a jug and threw it from the attic to the ground. Stunned by the noise, the sages stopped their prayers momentarily, and in the intervening moment, Rabbi Yehudah's soul departed.

Implications of Text 7:

OUR PRAYERS
Aliza Marton, acrylic and resin on wood panel, 2020, Los Angeles

TEXT 8

Preserving Each Moment

Maimonides, *Mishneh Torah*, Laws of Shabbat 2:1–18

דְחוּיָה הִיא שַׁבָּת אֵצֶל סַכָּנַת נְפָשׁוֹת כִּשְׁאַר כָּל הַמִּצְוֹת, לְפִיכָךְ חוֹלֶה שֶׁיֵּשׁ בּוֹ סַכָּנָה עוֹשִׂין לוֹ כָּל צְרָכָיו בְּשַׁבָּת עַל פִּי רוֹפֵא אֻמָּן שֶׁל אוֹתוֹ מָקוֹם . . .

מִי שֶׁנָּפְלָה עָלָיו מַפֹּלֶת, סָפֵק הוּא שָׁם סָפֵק אֵינוֹ שָׁם, מְפַקְּחִין עָלָיו. מְצָאוּהוּ חַי, אַף עַל פִּי שֶׁנִּתְרוֹצֵץ וְאִי אֶפְשָׁר שֶׁיַּבְרִיא, מְפַקְּחִין עָלָיו וּמוֹצִיאִין אוֹתוֹ לְחַיֵּי אוֹתָהּ שָׁעָה.

Shabbat laws are suspended in the face of danger to life, as are all other *mitzvot*. Consequently, we follow the direction of a professional physician on hand and attend to all of the patient's needs on Shabbat. . . .

If a structure collapses on Shabbat, the rubble must be cleared if there is even a doubt as to whether a person is beneath the debris [although clearing rubble is otherwise forbidden on Shabbat]. If a person is discovered alive, even if they are injured and crushed to the extent that it is impossible for them to recover, we must continue clearing the debris to extricate them, in the interest of preserving life for a short time.

RABBI MOSHE BEN MAIMON (MAIMONIDES, RAMBAM) 1135–1204

Halachist, philosopher, author, and physician. Maimonides was born in Córdoba, Spain. After the conquest of Córdoba by the Almohads, he fled Spain and eventually settled in Cairo, Egypt. There, he became the leader of the Jewish community and served as court physician to the vizier of Egypt. He is most noted for authoring the *Mishneh Torah*, an encyclopedic arrangement of Jewish law; and for his philosophical work, *Guide for the Perplexed*. His rulings on Jewish law are integral to the formation of Halachic consensus.

Implications of Text 8:

LIFE CYCLE
Michoel Muchnik, acrylics, pens, and ink, illustration from Joseph H. Hertz (ed.), *Sayings of the Fathers: Pirkei Avos* (West Orange, N.J.: Behrman House Publishing), 1986

TEXT 9

Life at All Costs

Rabbi Eliezer Yehudah Waldenberg, *Tzitz Eliezer* 18:62

פּוּק חָזֵי הֲלָכָה מְפֹרֶשֶׁת בְּשֻׁלְחָן עָרוּךְ (אֹרַח חַיִּים שכט, ד) דִּמְחַלְּלִין אֶת הַשַּׁבָּת אֲפִלּוּ עַל מִי שֶׁמְּצָאוּהוּ מְרֻצָּץ וְאֵינוֹ יָכוֹל לִחְיוֹת אֶלָּא לְפִי שָׁעָה, עַיֵּן שָׁם. וְהַמְרֻצָּץ הַזֶּה, הֲרֵי בְּוַדַּאי עַל יְדֵי הַגָּשַׁת הַטִּפּוּל לְחַיֵּי הַשָּׁעָה שֶׁלּוֹ יַאֲרִיכוּ עַל יְדֵי כֵּן גַּם כֵּן אֶת סִבְלוֹ. וּבְכָל זֹאת יֵשׁ חִיּוּב לַעֲשׂוֹת מַאֲמַצִּים לְהַאֲרִיךְ אֶת הַחַיֵּי שָׁעָה שֶׁלּוֹ כְּכָל הָאֶפְשָׁר . . .

וְאִם כָּכָה בְּשַׁבָּת, מִכָּל שֶׁכֵּן שֶׁיֵּשׁ חִיּוּב עַל כָּךְ בִּימוֹת הַחוֹל לַעֲשׂוֹת מַאֲמַצִּים לְהַצִּיל גַּם שֶׁכָּאֵלֶּה, וּלְהָשִׁיב לָהֶם חַיּוּת עַצְמִי, וְלוּ לְחַיֵּי שָׁעָה בִּלְבַד, וְגַם לְרַבּוֹת אֲפִלּוּ כְּשֶׁזֶּה כָּרוּךְ בְּסֵבֶל.

Jewish law asserts that we violate the laws of Shabbat even for the sake of one who is severely injured and can only live a little while longer. When we extricate this person, we inevitably prolong their suffering. Nevertheless, we are obligated to make every effort to prolong their life. . . .

If this is so on Shabbat, certainly on a weekday we are obliged to make every effort to prolong life, even for a brief duration, and even if this entails additional suffering.

RABBI ELIEZER YEHUDAH WALDENBERG
1915–2006

Noted Halachic authority. Rabbi Waldenberg served as judge on the Supreme Rabbinical Court in Jerusalem and was known as an eminent authority on Jewish medical ethics and Jewish law. He published his Halachic responsa, *Tzitz Eliezer*, which is viewed as one of the great achievements of Halachic scholarship of the 20th century. He served as rabbi for the Shaare Zedek Medical Center in Jerusalem.

Are there any permissible forms of euthanasia? World renowned decisor of Jewish law **Rabbi Hershel Schachter** responds: **myjli.com/decisions**

TEXT 10A

Withholding Treatment

Rabbi Moshe Feinstein, *Igrot Moshe, Choshen Mishpat* 2, 74:1

שֶׁאִם אֵין יוֹדְעִין הָרוֹפְאִים שׁוּם רְפוּאָה, לֹא רַק לְרַפְּאֹתוֹ אֶלָּא אַף לֹא לְהָקֵל הַיִּסוּרִין, אֶלָּא לְהַאֲרִיךְ קְצָת חַיָּיו כְּמוֹ שֶׁהֵן בְּהַיִּסוּרִין - אֵין לָהֶם לִתֵּן רְפוּאוֹת כָּאֵלוּ. שֶׁהֲרֵי בִּכְהַאי גַוְנָא חָזִינַן מֵעֻבְדָא דְרַבִּי (כְּתֻבּוֹת קד, א) שֶׁלֹּא הוֹעִילוּ רַבָּנָן בִּתְפִלָּתָם שֶׁיִּתְרַפֵּא וְגַם לֹא לְסַלֵּק יִסּוּרָיו, אֶלָּא שֶׁהוֹעִילָה תְּפִלָּתָם שֶׁלֹּא יָמוּת וְיִחְיֶה בְּהַיִּסוּרִים כְּמוֹ שֶׁהֵם כָּל זְמַן שֶׁמִּתְפַּלְּלִין. אָמְרָה אַמְתֵיה דְרַבִּי שֶׁהָיְתָה חֲכָמָה בַּתּוֹרָה: יְהִי רָצוֹן שֶׁיָּכוֹפוּ הָעֶלְיוֹנִים אֶת הַתַּחְתּוֹנִים. וּכְשֶׁרָאֲתָה שֶׁלֹּא הוֹעִילָה תְּפִלָּתָהּ מֵחֲמַת שֶׁלֹּא פָּסְקוּ רַבָּנָן מִלְּמִיבָּעֵי רַחֲמֵי, עָשְׂתָה מַעֲשֶׂה לְהַשְׁתִּיקָם מִתְּפִלָּתָם בִּשְׁבִירַת כּוּזָא וְנָח נַפְשֵׁיה.

וּמַשְׁמַע מֵהַגְּמָרָא שֶׁהוּבָא זֶה לְהוֹרוֹת הֲלָכָה שֶׁשַּׁפִּיר עָשְׂתָה . . . יֵשׁ לָנוּ לְמֵילַף לְחוֹלֶה שֶׁהָרוֹפְאִים אֵין יוֹדְעִין שׁוּם רְפוּאָה לְרַפְּאֹתוֹ, וְאַף לֹא לְהָקֵל הַיִּסוּרִין, רַק שֶׁיּוֹדְעִין מֵרְפוּאָה לְהַאֲרִיךְ קְצָת חַיָּיו בְּהַיִּסוּרִין כְּמוֹ שֶׁהֵם עַתָּה, שֶׁאֵין לִתֵּן רְפוּאוֹת כָּאֵלוּ . . . וְרַק אִם נִשְׁקַט רוּחוֹ דְּהַחוֹלֶה בְּמָה שֶׁיִּתֵּן לוֹ הָרוֹפֵא אֵיזֶה דָבָר, צָרִיךְ לִתֵּן לוֹ.

If physicians can neither cure a patient nor ease their suffering, they should not administer treatments that only serve to prolong briefly the terminal patient's life in suffering. We infer this from the Talmud's description of Rabbi Yehudah's final

RABBI MOSHE FEINSTEIN 1895–1986

Leading Halachic authority of the 20th century. Rabbi Feinstein was appointed rabbi of Luban, Belarus, in 1921. He immigrated to the U.S. in 1937 and became the dean of Metivta Tiferet Yerushalayim in New York. Rabbi Feinstein's Halachic decisions have been published in a multivolume collection entitled *Igrot Moshe*.

illness. The sages' prayers did not produce a cure for Rabbi Yehudah or lessen his agony, but only prolonged his ordeal for as long as they continued to pray. Rabbi Yehudah's maid, who was knowledgeable in Torah, said, "May it be Your will that those above prevail over those below." Upon seeing that her prayers could not be effective as long as the sages continued their supplications, she took a jug and smashed it in order to silence them. At that moment, Rabbi Yehudah passed away.

This incident is cited in the Talmud to teach us that the maid acted correctly. . . . We can derive from this that a physician should not administer to a patient a treatment that will neither cure them nor alleviate their torment but will serve only to prolong their life for a short duration in agony. . . . The physician should only administer such treatment if it will soothe the patient.

Detail from a donation receipt issued by The General Bikur Cholim Hospitals, Jerusalem, c. 1925 (Yeshiva University Museum, New York, N.Y.)

TEXT 10B

Between Natural Care and Treatment

Rabbi Moshe Feinstein, *Igrot Moshe, Choshen Mishpat* 2, 74:3

בִּתְשׁוּבָתִי לְהָרוֹפְאִים כָּתַבְתִּי שֶׁלְחוֹלֶה מְסֻכָּן שֶׁאֵינוֹ יָכוֹל לִנְשֹׁם צָרִיךְ לִתֵּן לוֹ חַמְצָן (אָקְסִידְזְשֶׁען), אַף שֶׁהוּא בְּאֹפֶן שֶׁאִי אֶפְשָׁר לְרַפְּאֹתוֹ, שֶׁהֲרֵי הוּא לְהָקֵל מִיִּסּוּרָיו, דְהַיִּסּוּרִין מִמָּה שֶׁאִי אֶפְשָׁר לִנְשֹׁם הֵם יִסּוּרִים גְדוֹלִים, וְהַחַמְצָן מְסַלְקָן.

וּכְפִי זֶה שָׁאַל כְּבוֹד תּוֹרָתוֹ הָרָמָה, אִם בְּחוֹלִים שֶׁאֵינָם יְכוֹלִין לֶאֱכֹל, אִם צְרִיכִין לִתֵּן לְהוּ אֹכֶל דֶרֶךְ הַוְּרִידִין כְּשֶׁהוּא מְסֻכָּן, שֶׁהוּא לְהַאֲרִיךְ חַיָּיו כְּמוֹ שֶׁהֵן בְּיִסּוּרִין, כְּשֶׁנִדְמֶה לָנוּ שֶׁאֵין לוֹ יִסּוּרִין מִמָּה שֶׁאֵינוֹ אֹכֵל.

פָּשׁוּט שֶׁצָרִיךְ לְהַאֲכִילוֹ דְבָרִים שֶׁאֵין מַזִיקִין וְאֵין מְקַלְקְלִין, דְוַדַאי מַחֲזִיקִין כֹּחוֹ מְעַט, אַף שֶׁהַחוֹלֶה בְּעַצְמוֹ אֵינוֹ מַרְגִישׁ, וְאַף הָעוֹמְדִין וּמְשַׁמְשִׁין אוֹתוֹ אֵין מַרְגִישִׁין. וְלֹא דָמִי כְּלַל לְעִנְיָנֵי סַמֵי רְפוּאָה, וְהַטַעַם פָּשׁוּט: שֶׁהָאֲכִילָה הוּא דָבָר טִבְעִי, שֶׁמֻכְרָחִין לֶאֱכֹל לְהַחֲזִיק הַחִיוּת וְשֵׂכֶל אָדָם.

In my responsum to the physicians, I wrote that one should administer oxygen to a terminally ill patient who has trouble breathing even though no cure will result, because it eases the patient's suffering; for inability to breathe is tremendously painful.

Accordingly, you asked regarding a terminally ill patient who is unable to eat normally: Should we intravenously feed him and thus extend his life while prolonging his suffering, when it appears that he has no pain in abstaining from food?

[My response:] Clearly, we must feed the patient, provided that it will not cause any harm, for food surely strengthens the patient somewhat, despite the possibility that neither the patient nor his attendants are aware of this effect. There is no need, however, to provide medicine [with the assumption that it too will strengthen the patient] and the distinction is obvious: eating is a natural need that is required to strengthen one's body and mind.

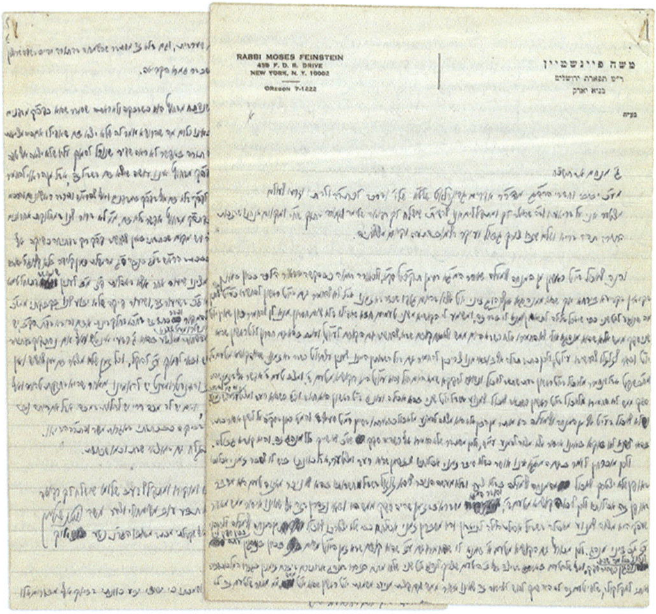

RABBI MOSES FEINSTEIN
455 F. D. R. DRIVE
NEW YORK, N. Y. 10002
ORegon 7-1222

משה פיינשטיין
ר״מ תפארת ירושלים
בנוא יארק

בע״ה

Rabbi Moshe Feinstein, handwritten responsum (letter of reply to a Halachic query), on Rabbi Feinstein's official letterhead, to his student Rabbi Efraim Greenblatt; includes a blessing for "complete and total recovery."

TEXT 11

Between the Ordinary and the Extraordinary

Professor Abraham S. Abraham, *Nishmat Avraham, Yoreh De'ah* 339:4

אָמַר לִי הַגָּאוֹן רַבִּי שְׁלֹמֹה זַלְמָן אוֹיֶערְבַּאךְ, זֵכֶר צַדִּיק לִבְרָכָה:

שֶׁצְּרִיכִים לְהַבְדִּיל בֵּין טִפּוּלִים הַמְמַלְאִים צְרָכָיו הַטִּבְעִיִּים שֶׁל הַחוֹלֶה אוֹ הַמְקֻבָּלִים כִּשְׁגְרָתִיִּים, וּבֵין טִפּוּלִים שֶׁהֵם מִחוּץ לְגֶדֶר הַשִּׁגְרָה.

וְלָכֵן חוֹלֶה, לְמָשָׁל, הַסּוֹבֵל מִסַּרְטָן שֶׁהִתְפַּשֵּׁט בְּגוּפוֹ וְהוּא קָרוֹב לְמִיתָה, עַל אַף שֶׁיֵּשׁ לוֹ יִסּוּרִים וּכְאֵבִים קָשִׁים, אָסוּר לְהַפְסִיק לוֹ אוֹ לִמְנֹעַ מִמֶּנּוּ חַמְצָן, אוֹ כָּל מָזוֹן אוֹ נוֹזֵל מֵזִין אַחֵר לָהֶם הוּא זָקוּק. אִם הוּא סוֹבֵל מִסֻּכֶּרֶת, אֵין לְהַפְסִיק אֶת מַתַּן הָאִינְסוּלִין כְּדֵי שֶׁיָּמוּת יוֹתֵר מַהֵר. אֵין לְהַפְסִיק אֶת מַתַּן דָּם אוֹ כָּל תְּרוּפָה אַחֶרֶת, כְּגוֹן אַנְטִיבְּיוֹטִיקָה, הַדְּרוּשָׁה לְטִפּוּלוֹ . . .

אוּלָם מֵאִידָךְ, אֵין כָּל חִיּוּב לְטַפֵּל בְּחוֹלֶה כָּזֶה בְּצוּרַת "קוּם וַעֲשֵׂה" - כְּשֶׁהַטִּפּוּל עַצְמוֹ יִגְרֹם לוֹ לִסְבֹּל רַב בְּנוֹסָף לְיִסּוּרָיו, כְּשֶׁהַטִּפּוּל הוּא מִחוּץ לְגֶדֶר הַשִּׁגְרָה, וּכְשֶׁאֵין לְצַפּוֹת אֶלָּא לְהַאֲרָכַת חַיָּיו בְּמִדַּת מָה, וְלֹא לְרִפּוּי מַחֲלָתוֹ הַיְסוֹדִית, וּבִמְיֻחָד אִם גַּם הַחוֹלֶה אֵינוֹ מַסְכִּים, עֵקֶב הַכְּאֵבִים הַקָּשִׁים אוֹ הַסֵּבֶל הָרַב.

ABRAHAM S. ABRAHAM M.D., FRCP

Physician, author, and medical ethicist. Dr. Abraham was born in Jerusalem and received his medical training in England. Since 1989, he has been chief of internal medicine at the Shaare Zedek Medical Center in Jerusalem, and since 1990, a professor of medicine at the Hebrew University Hadassah Medical School. His most notable work, *Nishmat Avraham,* printed in both Hebrew and English, is an essential text addressing medical-Halachic issues.

Rabbi Shlomo Zalman Auerbach of righteous memory told me the following:

There is a difference between treatments that satisfy the natural needs of a patient—or those considered ordinary treatments; and those that are considered extraordinary treatments.

For example, if a patient suffers from metastasized cancer and is about to die, although they are in pain, we may not withhold the required oxygen, nutrition, and hydration. If they suffer from diabetes, we may not withhold insulin with the intention that they die sooner. Blood transfusions and any other medication that the patient requires, such as antibiotics, should not be withheld. . . .

On the other hand, there is no obligation to initiate an extraordinary medical procedure, that is, a procedure that would itself cause much pain (in addition to the pain that this patient already experiences) if this treatment has no chance of curing the underlying disease but only of extending life for a short duration.

FIGURE 2.2

Contemporary Halachic Positions Regarding Care for Terminally Ill People

	RABBI MOSHE FEINSTEIN	RABBI SHLOMO ZALMAN AUERBACH	RABBI ELIEZER WALDENBERG
PHYSICIAN-ASSISTED SUICIDE	No	No	No
REMOVING A RESPIRATOR OR ANYTHING ELSE KEEPING THE PERSON ALIVE	No	No	No
DECLINING HYDRATION, NUTRITION, AND OXYGEN	No	No	No
DECLINING NON-PAINFUL, LIFE-EXTENDING TREATMENT	Yes	No	No
DECLINING PAINFUL MEDICAL TREATMENT	Yes	Yes	No

IV. ADVANCE MEDICAL DIRECTIVES

This section provides insight into the general guidance of Jewish law regarding practical end-of-life scenarios.

TEXT 12

The Health-Care Proxy

Rabbi Yitzchak Breitowitz, "The Right to Die: A Halachic Approach," www.jlaw.com

The living will, however, which attempts to spell out in advance which treatments should be employed and which should not, is too blunt of an instrument to accurately mirror the necessary value judgments. The basis for all of these decisions is the pain and suffering the patient feels at the time of the illness, and this can simply not be predicted in advance. Conditions that may seem intolerable to us when we are 35–40 may be quite adequate when we reach 85 and we realize that the alternative would be death. Keep in mind too that many patients, such as those with advanced Alzheimer's or in comas, may in fact not be suffering, though their existence is undoubtedly a hardship to their families. Moreover, it is almost impossible to spell out all contingencies in advance, making living wills incomplete almost by definition.

Far preferable to the living will is the durable power of attorney (often called a health-care proxy) which simply specifies a person—family member, friend, clergyman—empowered to make health-care decisions on the patient's behalf in the event he or she is incapacitated. The power may in addition specify that all decisions shall be made in accordance with Jewish law and in consultation with a designated clergyman of the patient's choice. . . . This document insures that decisions will be made consistently with the moral and religious beliefs that the patient holds dear. Obviously, one should discuss these delicate matters ahead of time both with family members and spiritual advisers.

For a sample of a halachic health-care proxy form provided by the Rabbinical Council of America, see Addendum.

TEXT 13

DNR Side Effects

Mary Catherine Beach and R. Sean Morrison, "The Effect of Do-Not-Resuscitate Orders on Physician Decision-Making," *Journal of American Geriatrics Society* 50:12 (2002), p. 2057

The effect of do-not-resuscitate (DNR) orders on physicians' decisions to provide life-prolonging treatments other than cardiopulmonary resuscitation (CPR) for patients near the end of life was explored. . . . The presence of a DNR order may affect physicians' willingness to order a variety of treatments not related to CPR. Patients with DNR orders may choose to forgo other life-prolonging treatments, but physicians should elicit additional information about patients' treatment goals to inform these decisions.

TRATADO
sobre MEDECINA que
fez oDoutor ZACUTO
para seu filho levar consigo
quando se foy para oBrazil,

Disposto, eCopeado,
por horden de
Ishack de Matatia Aboab,

Anno 5450:

Escrito por B. Godines.

Title page of Portuguese medical book, *Tratado sobre Medicina–Short Treatise on Medicine*, by Marrano physician Avraham Zacuto, copied (for his son, Isaac Matatiah Aboab, to take to Brazil) by Jewish Dutch engraver Benjamin Senior Godines, Amsterdam, 1690 (Ets Haim Library, Portuguese Synagogue of Amsterdam)

Whose life is it, anyway? **Rabbi Yitzchak Schochet** gives fascinating insight into Judaism's approach to some of the hot topics of modern-day moral dilemmas: **myjli.com/decisions**

KEY POINTS

1. Each human is created in the image of G-d. Terminating a human life, even for seemingly benevolent purposes, desecrates that image and profanes the person's inherent sanctity. Jewish law therefore prohibits physician-assisted suicide and any act that will lead directly to a patient's death.

2. Using a human frame of reference, life, at times, might seem futile. Judaism teaches that every moment of life pulsates with spiritual purpose and potential. Embracing a mission-oriented mindset helps us cherish each moment and its unique mission, despite any hardship.

3. Purpose can be found in a single moment of repentance and good deeds. In addition, the luminosity of the human soul has a significant spiritual impact on its environment.

4. The Jewish approach to end-of-life care is guided by two considerations: the desire to ameliorate pain and suffering, and the belief in the value of life's every moment. The various views about withholding care seek to balance these two factors.

5. There are instances in which there is no halachic obligation to administer certain treatments to terminally ill patients. Due to the nuances of this topic, it is optimal that one's advance medical directive should specify that all decisions should be made in consultation with a clergyman of the patient's choice.

Why Did King Saul Commit Suicide?

Toward the end of the first Book of Samuel, we read of the Jewish army's disastrous battle against invading Philistines. King Saul was surrounded, but rather than allow himself to be captured by the enemy, he deliberately fell on his sword. While some commentators argue that Saul's actions were inappropriate, the majority of opinions consider his suicide Halachically acceptable. Understanding the approval of this act is vitally important, because it addresses a larger question of whether there are any extreme circumstances under which choosing to end one's life can be justified.

We present here the biblical narrative of Saul's suicide, complemented with several explanations of his action.

I SAMUEL 31:1–4

1 The Philistines battled Israel, and
the Israelites fled before them and
many fell slain on Mount Gilboa. The
Philistines overtook Saul and his
sons, and they killed Saul's sons—
Jonathan, Abinadab, and Malkishua.

2 The fighting grew fierce around
Saul. The Philistine archers found
him, and he was terrified.

3 Saul told his weapon-bearer, "Draw
your sword and run me through with
it, or else these heathens will come
and run me through and abuse me."
The weapon-bearer was unwilling;
he was extremely afraid.

4 Saul took the sword and fell on it.

Averting Mass Fatalities

Rabbi Shlomo Luria, *Yam Shel Shlomo*, Bava Kama 8:59

No matter how afraid a person may be of the consequences of staying alive, it is forbidden to commit suicide. . . . This holds true even for an individual who has been captured and fears they will be tortured until they succumb and agree to perform an act of idolatry. . . .

However, suicide is permitted for an individual who fears that he will be tortured to divulge incriminating information about other innocent Jews and thereby cause the deaths of many others. This is indeed the unfortunate practice of certain unscrupulous rulers—they torture a Jew to extract a false confession that fatally implicates an entire Jewish community.

This may have been King Saul's rationale for throwing himself onto his own sword; he reasoned that if he were captured alive, he would be humiliated and tortured. Presumably, the Jewish people would not sit idly by in the face of their king's public suffering, and they would attempt to avenge his honor and rescue him. Tens of thousands of additional lives would be lost in the process.

Avoiding Sexual Abuse

Rabbi Avraham Yitzchak Hakohen Kook, *Mishpat Kohen* 144:4

Rabbi Asher ben Yechiel argues that King Saul feared that the Philistines would sexually abuse him. The verse reports that he feared "abuse" at the hands of his captors, and the identical term is used elsewhere in the Bible (Judges 19:25) to connote rape. This teaches us that it is permissible to commit suicide to avoid being subjected to rape.

Avoiding Forced Idolatry

Rabbi Yomtov Asevilli (Ritva), Avodah Zarah 18a

Rabbeinu Tam stated that one may take their own life if they fear being coerced to convert to another religion.

The Torah tells us, "However [*ach*], for your own lifeblood, I will demand an accounting" (Genesis 9:5). The Midrash expounds, "This teaches us that we may not take our own life." The Midrash continues, "We might conclude that King Saul was wrong for falling on his sword. To counter this, the Torah prefaced the prohibition with the limiting term '*ach*,' which teaches us that in Saul's case this was permissible." Rabbeinu Tam explained that the reason it was permissible for Saul to take his own life was because he would have been forced into idolatry had he been captured by the Philistines alive. . . .

Nevertheless, to determine whether this conclusion is correct requires further study.

Protecting G-d's Honor

Rabbi Shlomo Luria, *Yam Shel Shlomo*, Bava Kama 8:59

It is also possible that Saul reasoned that it is unbecoming and dishonorable for the king—G-d's anointed—to be tortured and to suffer a humiliating death at the hands of the Philistines. This would have been an enormous desecration of G-d's name and a public humiliation of the Jewish faith.

Addendum: Halachic Living Will

The Rabbinical Council of America

Halachic Health Care Proxy

Proxy and Directive With Respect To Health Care and Post-Mortem Decisions

Introduction

This Halachic Health Care Proxy, revised in August of 2009, is designed to help ensure that all medical and post-death decisions made by others on your behalf will be made in accordance with Jewish law and custom (*Halacha*). **This document is of great importance in light of in-roads made by medical service providers to insert themselves into the decision making process of patients and their families regarding end-of-life issues**. The text of this Halachic Health Care Proxy has been approved by attorneys. While we do not expect that any future change in federal or state laws would materially affect the validity of this document, you should show it to your own attorney to confirm its effectiveness in your state and for your specific needs.

Acknowledgment

The Rabbinical Council of America wishes to acknowledge the pioneering work of Agudath Israel of America, whose Health Care Proxy was invaluable in the formulation of this document.

Further Guidelines

The RCA has also prepared a separate document titled **"Halachic Guidelines to Assist Patients and their Families in Making 'End-of-Life' Medical Decisions"** which should be reviewed prior to filling out this form. Like this document, it is available for download at www.rabbis.org (and in printed form can be found at the back of this document.)

Halachic Health Care Proxy Registration

The Union of Orthodox Jewish Congregations of America, through an agreement with the New York Legal Assistance Group (NYLAG), has arranged registration of your Halachic Health Care Proxy free of charge with the U.S. Living Will Registry. The Registry will maintain a copy on a secure website that can be accessed instantly by healthcare providers around the country 24 hours a day through its automated service. We encourage registration, because, in many instances, a patient has to be rushed to the hospital and the family may not be able to locate or access the health care proxy.

Registrants will receive confirmation of their registration and labels to affix to their insurance card & driver's license, stating that their advance directive is registered, and a wallet card listing their Registration #. The registrant is contacted annually by mail to confirm that the advance directive has not been changed or revoked, and to update personal and emergency contact information. This annual update is included in this life-time registration; there is never a charge to the registrant for annual updates or for continued registration.

For more detailed information on the registry, see www.oucommunity.org

---

The Rabbinical Council of America

305 Seventh Avenue, New York, NY 10001

www.rabbis.org

Instructions

(a) Print your name on the first line of the form.

(b) In Section 1, print the name, address, and telephone numbers of the person you wish to designate as your agent to make medical decisions on your behalf if you ever become incapable of making them on your own. Be sure to include all numbers (including cell phone and pager) where your agent can be reached in the event of an emergency. If the contact information for your agent changes, you should provide that updated information to everyone whom you have provided with a copy of your Health Care Proxy.

You should also insert the name, address, and telephone numbers of an alternate agent, to make such decisions if your main agent is unable, unwilling, or unavailable to make such decisions.

Before appointing anyone to serve as your agent, or alternate agent, ascertain that person's willingness to serve in such capacity. For your convenience, an addendum at the end of this document provides talking points to facilitate discussion between you and your proxy. In addition, if you have made arrangements with a burial society (*Chevra Kadisha*) for the handling and disposition of your body after death, you may wish to advise your agents of such arrangements.

Note: the law allows virtually any competent adult (an adult is a person 18 years of age or older, or anyone who has married) to serve as a health care agent. Thus, you may appoint as your agent (or alternate agent) your spouse, adult child, parent or other adult relative.

You may also appoint a non-relative to serve as your agent (or alternate agent), provided that individual has not already been appointed by 10 other persons to serve as a health care agent, or, is a non-physician employee of a health care facility in which you are a patient or resident.

(c) In Section 3, please print the name(s), addresses, and telephone numbers of the Orthodox rabbi and the alternate Orthodox rabbi whose guidance you want your agent to follow, should any questions arise as to the requirements of *halacha*.

You are free to insert the name of any Orthodox Rabbi(s) you choose. However, you are encouraged to discuss the matter with the rabbi to ascertain his specialization in end-of-life halachic issues and willingness to serve in such capacity.

(d) In Section 8, sign and print your name, address, phone numbers, and the date. If you are not physically able to sign and date the form, the law allows another person to do so on your behalf, as long as he or she does so at your direction, in your presence, and in the presence of two adult witnesses.

(e) In the Declaration of Witnesses section, two witnesses should sign their names and insert their addresses beneath your signature. These two witnesses must be competent adults. Neither of them should be the person you have appointed as your health care agent (or alternate agent). They may, however, be your relatives.

If you reside in a mental health facility, at least one witness must be an individual who is not affiliated with the facility. In addition, if the mental health facility is also a hospital, at least one witness must be a qualified psychiatrist.

(f) It is recommended that you keep the original of this form among your valuable papers in a location that is readily accessible in the event of an emergency; and that you distribute copies to the health care agent (and alternate agent) you have designated in section 1, to the rabbi(s) you have designated in section 3, as well as to your doctors, your lawyer, and anyone else who is likely to be contacted in times of emergency.

(g) If, at any time, you wish to revoke this Proxy and Directive, you may do so by executing a new one; or by notifying your agent or health care provider, in writing, of your intent to revoke it. To avoid possible confusion, it would be wise to try to obtain all originals and copies of the old Proxy and Directive and destroy them.

If you do not revoke the Proxy and Directive, the Law provides that it remains in effect indefinitely. Obviously, if any of the persons whose names you have inserted in the Proxy and Directive dies or becomes otherwise incapable of serving in the role you have assigned, you should execute a new Proxy and Directive.

(h) It is recommended that you also complete the Emergency Instructions Card contained at the end of this form, and carry it with you in your wallet or purse.

(i) If, upon consultation with your rabbi, you would like to add to this standardized Proxy and Directive any additional expression of your wishes with respect to medical and/or post-mortem decisions, you may do so by attaching a "rider" to the standardized form. If you choose to do so, or if you have any other questions concerning this form, please consult an attorney.

These instructions are not part of the Halachic Health Care Proxy and need not be kept attached to the executed document.

Proxy and Directive With Respect To Health Care Decisions and Post-Mortem Decisions

I, ____, hereby declare as follows:

1. Appointment of Agent: In recognition of the fact that there may come a time when I will become unable to make my own health care decisions because of illness, injury or other circumstances, I hereby appoint

Agent

Name ____

Address ____

Telephone/Email:

Office____________________ **Home** ______________________

Cell ____________________ **E-mail:** ______________________

as my health care agent to make any and all health care decisions for me, consistent with my wishes as set forth in this directive. If the person named above is unable, unwilling or unavailable to act as my agent, I hereby appoint

Alternate Agent

Name ____

Address____

Telephone/Email:

Office____________________ **Home** ______________________

Cell ____________________ **E-mail:** ______________________

to serve in such capacity.

This appointment shall take effect in the event I become unable, because of illness, injury or other circumstances, to make my own health care decisions.

2. Jewish Law to Govern Health Care Decisions: I am Jewish. It is my desire, and I hereby direct, that all health care decisions made for me (whether made by my agent, a guardian appointed for me, or any other person) be made pursuant to Jewish law and custom as determined in accordance with Orthodox interpretation and tradition. Without limiting in any way the generality of the foregoing, it is my wish that Jewish Law and custom should dictate the course of my health care with respect to such matters as the performance of cardio-pulmonary resuscitation if I suffer cardiac or respiratory arrest; the performance of life-sustaining surgical procedures and the initiation or maintenance of any particular course of life-sustaining medical treatment or other form of life-support maintenance, including the provision of nutrition and hydration; and the criteria by which death shall be determined, including the method by which such criteria shall be medically ascertained or confirmed.

3. Ascertaining the Requirements of Jewish Law: In determining the requirements of Jewish law and custom in connection with this declaration, I direct my agent to consult with the following Orthodox Rabbi and I ask my agent to comply with his halachic decisions:

Rabbi

Name____

Address____

Telephone/Email:

Office__________________________ **Home** ________________________________

Cell __________________________ **E-mail:** ______________________________

If such Orthodox Rabbi is unable, unwilling or unavailable to provide such consultation and guidance, I direct my agent to consult with the following Orthodox Rabbi and I ask my agent to comply with his halachic decisions:

Alternate Rabbi

Name____

Address ____

Telephone/Email:

Office__________________________ **Home** ________________________________

Cell __________________________ **E-mail:** ______________________________

4. Direction to Health Care Providers: Any health care provider shall rely upon and carry out the decisions of my agent, and may assume that such decisions reflect my wishes and were arrived at in accordance with the procedures set forth in this directive, unless such health care provider shall have good cause to believe that my agent has not acted in good faith in accordance with my wishes as expressed in this directive.

If the persons designated in section 1 above as my agent and alternate agent are unable, unwilling or unavailable to serve in such capacity, it is my desire, and I hereby direct, that any health care provider or other person who will be making health care decisions on my behalf follow the procedures outlined in section 3 above in determining the requirements of Jewish law and custom.

Pending contact with the agent and/or Orthodox Rabbi described above, it is my desire, and I hereby direct, that all health care providers undertake all essential emergency and/or life sustaining measures on my behalf.

5. Access to Medical Records and Information; HIPAA: My agent(s) and Rabbi(s) are hereby authorized under the Health Insurance Portability and Accountability Act of 1996 ("HIPAA") access to any and all protected information, and accordingly all of my protected health information (as such term is defined under HIPAA) and other medical records shall be made available to my agent and rabbi upon request in the same manner as such information and records would be released and disclosed to me, and my agent and rabbi shall have and may exercise all of the rights I would have regarding the use and disclosure of such information and records, as required under HIPAA.

6. Post-Mortem Decisions: It is also my desire, and I hereby direct, that after my death, all decisions concerning the handling and disposition of my body be made pursuant to Jewish law and custom as determined in accordance with Orthodox interpretation and tradition. For example, Jewish law generally requires expeditious burial and imposes special requirements with regard to the preparation of the body for burial. It is my wish that Jewish law and custom be followed with respect to these matters.

Further, subject to certain limited exceptions, Jewish law generally prohibits the performance of any autopsy or dissection. It is my wish that Jewish law and custom be followed with respect to such procedures, and with respect to all other post-mortem matters including the removal and usage of any of my body organs or tissue for transplantation or any other purposes. I direct that any health care provider in attendance at my death notify the agent and/or Orthodox Rabbi described above immediately upon my death, in addition to any other person whose consent by law must be solicited and obtained, prior to the use of any part of my body as an anatomical gift, so that appropriate decisions and arrangements can be made in accordance with my wishes. Pending such notification, and unless there is specific authorization by the Orthodox Rabbi consulted in accordance with the procedures outlined in section 3 above, it is my desire, and I hereby direct, that no post-mortem procedure be performed on my body.

7. Incontrovertible Evidence of My Wishes: If, for any reason, this document is deemed not legally effective as a health care proxy, or if the persons designated in section 1 above as my agent and alternate agent are unable, unwilling or unavailable to serve in such capacity, I declare to my family, my doctor and anyone else whom it may concern that the wishes I have expressed herein with regard to compliance with Jewish law and custom should be treated as incontrovertible evidence of my intent and desire with respect to all health care measures and post-mortem procedures; and that it is my wish that the procedure outlined in section 3 above should be followed in determining the requirements of Jewish law and custom.

8. Duration and Revocation: It is my understanding and intention that unless I revoke this proxy and directive, it will remain in effect indefinitely. My signature on this document shall be deemed to constitute a revocation of any prior health care proxy, directive or other similar document I may have executed prior to today's date.

My Signature ______________________________
(If you are not physically able to sign, please ask another person to sign your name on your behalf.)

My Name (printed) ______________________________ **Date** ____________

Address ______________________________

____

Telephone/Email:

Office______________ **Home** ______________

Cell ______________ **E-mail:** ______________

Declaration of Witnesses

I, on this __________ day of __________, 20___, declare that the person who signed (or asked another to sign) this document is personally known to me and appears to be of sound mind and acting willingly and free from duress. He/She signed (or asked another to sign for him/her) this document in my presence (and that person signed in my presence). I am not the person appointed as agent by this document

Signature of Witness 1 ______________________________

Name (printed) ______________________________

Address ______________________________

____

Telephone/Email:

Office______________ **Home** ______________

Cell ______________ **E-mail:** ______________

Signature of Witness 2 ______________________________

Name (printed) ______________________________

Address ______________________________

____

Telephone/Email:

Office______________ **Home** ______________

Cell ______________ **E-mail:** ______________

Appendices

Expression of Intent

See Instructions paragraph (i)

The issues surrounding end-of-life medical decisions are critical and most complex. We, therefore, strongly recommend that you discuss your wishes and concerns openly with your Health Care proxy (as well as the alternate) and your designated Rabbi. In order to give them guidance, in the event that you are unable to make your own decisions, we ask you to review the following scenarios and discuss with them whether you wish to be treated aggressively with all appropriate life-support interventions, or palliative/comfort care, which may include pain medications, symptom relief, antibiotics and feeding tubes.

- *If I become terminally ill, I want to be treated.....*
- *If I am in a coma or have little conscious understanding, with no hope of recovery, then I want to be treated.....*
- *If I have brain damage or a brain disease that makes me unable to recognize people or speak and there is no hope that my condition will improve, I wish to be treated.....*

Medical technology is constantly advancing, so that new treatment options may become available in the future. Additionally, your advance directives at this time of your life may not necessarily apply if or when conditions change. We, therefore, urge you to periodically update this HCP, Health Care Proxy form, along with your DBA, Durable Power-of-Attorney, and Will.

Emergency Instructions Card

See Instructions paragraph (h)

Health Care Proxy
Emergency Instructions

I ______________________________________
have executed a "Halachic Health Care Proxy" (HCP) with respect to medical and post-mortem decisions, dated ________________. Pursuant to the Halachic HCP, the persons listed on the reverse of this card are to serve as my agent and alternate agent, respectively, in making health care decisions for me if I become unable to do so.

I desire that all such health care decisions, as well as all decisions relating to the handling and disposition of my body after I die, should be made pursuant to Jewish law and custom as determined in accordance with Orthodox interpretation and tradition. If there is any question regarding Jewish law and custom, my agent (or any other person making decisions for me) should consult with and follow the guidance of the rabbi or alternate rabbi identified on the reverse of this card. Pending contact with my agent I desire that health care providers should undertake all essential emergency measures on my behalf; and I desire that no autopsy, organ removal, or other post-mortem procedure be performed on my body without authorization from my agent.

Agent:______________________________

Phone: Office:____________ Home: ________________

Cell: ________________ E-Mail:________________

Alternate Agent: ______________________________

Phone: Office: ____________ Home: ______________

Cell: ______________ Email: __________________

Rabbi: ______________________________

Phone: Office____________ Home:______________

Cell:________________ E-mail________________

Alternate Rabbi ______________________________

Phone: Office:____________ Home:______________

Cell________________ E-Mail ________________

The Rabbinical Council of America
Halachic Guidelines to Assist Patients and their Families in Making "End-of-Life" Medical Decisions
As of August 10, 2009

This document is intended to provide general halachic guidance to patients and families involved in making difficult medical decisions that frequently arise at the end of life. It is not intended as a source for halachic decisions, nor is it a substitute for the essential dialogue among patients, families, rabbis and doctors. **All end-of-life issues and questions should be presented to a Halachic authority, preferably, when possible, before they become urgent or emergency decisions.**

1. What are Advance Directives?

Advance directives are guidelines about one's preferences for care in advance of a possible catastrophic event or change in one's mental capacity. The objective of these directives is to provide a person the opportunity to direct their care and share their preferences for treatment even if they are no longer able to participate in the decision-making process. Examples of such circumstances include stroke, coma or dementia.

There are two legal vehicles, or advance directives, that are used to facilitate decision-making when patients are not capable of making them. Both of these documents are used ***only*** in cases where the patients are deemed to be incapable to make their own decisions.

Living Will
This document details what to do in specific medical scenarios. Patients decide, in advance, which specific treatments they would request or refuse in each scenario.

Health Care Proxy
This document allows patients to choose an individual who will make decisions on their behalf in case they are unable to do so. While there are no case scenarios in this document, the patient can append specific requests to the document. In the ideal circumstance, the proxy should be intimately familiar with the patient's preferences for end-of- life treatment.

2. What is a halachic Advance Directive? How does it differ from similar documents?

While there are similarities in the nature of the forms, there are fundamental and profound differences between halachic and secular Advance Directives, especially the living will.

The ethical and philosophical underpinnings of secular Advance Directives are based on contemporary secular ethics. The halachic living will assumes adherence to the principles of the Torah as interpreted in the Orthodox tradition. Consequently, it is essential to consult with an Orthodox halachic authority to assure that Advance Directives are compliant with Orthodox tradition.

3. What is a Do Not Resuscitate (DNR) order? Is DNR ever permitted?

When patients with life threatening conditions are admitted to the hospital, they or their families will often be asked if they would like to sign a Do Not Resuscitate (DNR) order. This order means that that if the patient's heart stops beating, or if they stop breathing, the medical staff will not initiate CPR or any life-saving maneuvers. Jewish law emphatically emphasizes the preservation of life, though there may be circumstances when a DNR order would be halachicly appropriate.

As a word of caution, a DNR order can often be interpreted by the medical staff in a broader sense than intended. It may be perceived as an order to refrain from any aggressive therapy for the patient -- DNT, Do Not Treat. It is essential that the family clarifies their specific intentions and all limitations to the DNR order.

4. What is a Do Not Intubate (DNI) order? Is DNI ever permitted?

One of the treatments often utilized at the end of life is artificial (mechanical) respiration. The procedure for introducing a tube into the lungs, which aids in breathing, is called intubation. The tube is connected to a machine (called a ventilator, respirator, or life-support system). The family will be asked about intubation, either separately, or as a part of the DNR order. The medical indications for intubation are many and are **not** the same in every patient. As with the DNR order, there may be circumstances when it is halachicly appropriate to withhold intubation.

If artificial respiration (intubation) is withheld, in accordance with the ruling of a Halachic authority, oxygen supplementation via face mask or nasal prongs can still be provided. Oxygen is usually considered basic care and should be provided to all patients for whom it is medically indicated.

5. Once a patient has been placed on life support, can it ever be removed?

In Jewish law it is forbidden to perform an act that will directly result in the death of the patient. Therefore, removal of a respirator, when it will directly result in the patient's immediate death, is unequivocally prohibited. However, respirators are used for many reasons, and are safely removed in many situations. For patients at the end of life, it may be medically appropriate, in certain circumstances, to remove a respirator, as the respirator may not be required for the patient's care. **This area requires the input of medical and halachic expertise, and one should proceed with great caution.**

6. **How is nutrition delivered to terminal patients unable to take food by mouth? Must such "artificial" nutrition always be provided?**

Certain patients with terminal conditions may be unable to eat normally and may require artificial methods to deliver nutrition and hydration. These artificial means can include the following:

Nasogastric Tube (NG tube) – This is a plastic tube that is inserted into the nose (or mouth) and passed into the stomach. This procedure has few complications. It is usually a temporary (days/weeks) measure for delivering nutrition and hydration. Water and specially formulated nutritional liquids can be administered through this tube.

Total Parenteral Nutrition (TPN) - This requires the placement of a catheter (thin tube) into one of the major blood vessels of the body. Only specially designed liquids can be instilled into this catheter. This can be used for prolonged periods, but is not a permanent method of nutrition. There are some potential complications associated with the insertion and maintenance of TPN.

Percutaneous Endoscopic Gastrostomy (PEG) – This is a tube placed directly into the stomach. The term "feeding tube" is used commonly to refer to this device. This requires a minor procedure (endoscopy) with sedation. There are some potential complications associated with the insertion and maintenance of a PEG. This *can* be a permanent method of nutritional delivery. Pureed foods and pulverized pills can be administered through the PEG.

While secular wills include the option to refuse nutrition and hydration, generally Halacha assumes that nutrition should be delivered to all patients. Halachic authorities consider nutrition to be essential, and generally recommend its provision to all patients, whether conscious or comatose. However, there may be circumstances when artificial nutrition and hydration may be discontinued, in accordance with Halacha.

7. **Pain control and the use of morphine**

Narcotic pain medications, such as morphine, are often prescribed for terminal patients to alleviate suffering near life's end. These medications which provide pain relief are also associated with rare complications that may potentially hasten a patient's death. The alleviation of pain and suffering is a mitzvah and should not be withheld out of concern for potential adverse effects. It is clearly halachicly permitted for patients to receive narcotic medication, even when it may possibly hasten their death, when the following conditions are met:

- The intent is purely to alleviate suffering; *not* to terminate life.
- The dose of medicine is gradually increased as necessary to alleviate the pain.

8. **If someone suffers from a terminal condition, such as cancer, and develops a secondary infection (e.g., pneumonia or urinary tract infection), must the infection be treated?**

While Halachic authorities often require the treatment of secondary infections, there may be situations where treatment for secondary infections or complications may be halachicly withheld.

9. **Is brain death considered halachic death?**

The definition of death, one of the most complex issues in modern medical Halacha, is beyond the scope of this document. There are different halachic opinions as to whether "brain death" constitutes halachic death, and correspondingly, how treatment should proceed in these cases. Even the performance of diagnostic tests for the diagnosis or confirmation of brain death should be discussed with a halachic authority. .

10. **Is it permitted to be an organ donor (after death)?**

From a medical and legal perspective, organs can be donated from patients who are alive and well (e.g. kidneys, partial liver donation); have sustained cardiac death (e.g. eyes, skin, bone and possibly kidneys); or are brain dead (e.g. heart, liver, lung and kidney). The halachic approach to organ donation is varied and complex, and beyond the scope of this document. Questions about organ donation both before and after death should be posed to a halachic authority.

11. **Is an autopsy permitted?**

While autopsies are generally prohibited according to Jewish law, there are rare cases when they may be permitted. Modified autopsies or postmortem imaging should be considered where possible even in these cases.

Conclusion

All end-of-life issues and questions should be presented to a Halachic authority, preferably, when possible, before they become urgent or emergency decisions. The above guidelines are intended to provide general information regarding the approach of a Torah observant Jew towards making difficult end -of -life medical decisions. They are not decisive, nor comprehensive. All end-of-life cases should be discussed with a halachic authority. We strongly encourage direct and candid dialogue among the individual, their proxy and their halachic authority prior to completion of the document. In addition, we urge revisiting health care proxy documents on a periodic basis to assure that they are current.

LESSON 3

PREGNANCY QUESTIONS

Is a fetus a human life or a part of the mother's body? When pregnancy endangers a woman's life, may she, in good conscience, carry the pregnancy to term? Explore questions of pregnancy through the lens of Jewish texts.

PINK MELODY
Eduard Grossman
(1946–2017))

I. INTRODUCTION

The present lesson addresses the highly significant and equally sensitive topic of abortion. It presents and analyzes Jewish source texts indicating the circumstances under which abortion may be permitted or prohibited according to the principles of Jewish law—and suggests the ways this discussion might inform personal decisions in this difficult area. Note, however, that clarifying public policy regarding abortion is beyond the scope of the present lesson.

EXERCISE 3.1

The lesson video presents the dilemma of Ruchami, whose life is endangered by her pregnancy; nevertheless, she is adamantly set against terminating her pregnancy.

If you had to offer a personal opinion, would you consider it morally acceptable for Ruchami to risk her own life for the sake of saving her unborn child?

II. TALMUDIC EMBRYOLOGY

The first step toward evaluating Judaism's position on abortion is to analyze a Talmudic passage that offers insight into the Jewish philosophical view of an unborn fetus's status.

AFTER CHILDBIRTH
Etching by Philipp Gottfried Harder, German, c. 1731. The words below the etching mention Leviticus 12:2–5, which discusses the spiritual-purity status of a woman during the weeks after childbirth.

Life Lessons from the Womb

A cryptic Talmudic text uses rich and detailed imagery to describe the experience of a fetus in the womb. Scholars throughout the generations have explored this text and discovered layers of meaning and guidance.

Rabbi Simla'i taught that a fetus inside its mother's womb resembles a folded writing tablet: Its two hands rest on its temples, its two elbows rest on its knees, its heels rest against its buttocks, and its head lies between its knees. Its mouth is closed and its navel is open. ❶ It eats what its mother eats, drinks what its mother drinks, ❷ and produces no excrement. . . .

A lamp burns above its head and it sees from one end of the world to the other ❸ . . .

The fetus is taught the entire Torah ❹ . . . However, as the fetus emerges into the world, an angel approaches and strikes its mouth, ❺ causing it to forget the entire Torah. . . ❻

The fetus does not emerge before it is made to take an oath ❼ . . . What is the content of the oath? "Be righteous and not wicked. And even if the entire world says to you, 'You are righteous,' consider yourself as if you were wicked. ❽ And know that the Holy One, Blessed be He, is pure, and his servants are pure, and the soul He gave you is pure."

❶ There are life lessons to be learned from every detail of Rabbi Simla'i's depiction of the fetus's in-utero position.

Comparing the child's position to a writing tablet reflects our sages' repeated calls to always recall the principle of Divine accountability, such as, "The notebook is open and the hand is writing" (Avot 3:16), and "All your deeds are recorded in a book" (Avot 2:1). The child's hands rest on its temples, teaching that one's actions, symbolized by the hands, must be performed with the fullness of thought. Its legs are folded against its buttocks, indicating that while some allow themselves to be led wherever their feet lead them, the righteous actively control their lowest instincts. Its mouth is closed, reflecting the profound wisdom of silence. It is sustained through its navel that it situated at the body's midpoint, indicating that one should always maintain a balanced approach to consumption, whether in food, drink, or other matters.

Rabbi Yosef Chaim of Baghdad *(Ben Ish Chai), Ben Yehoyada*

❷ A fetus cannot select what it eats and drinks, but is instead sustained by that which its mother chooses to eat and drink. At birth, the newborn begins the process of serving G-d and making choices for itself by its own effort. The soul of the newborn celebrates its newfound ability to serve G-d through its own exertion, as an independent life. Although the child will not gain the formal obligation to perform *mitzvot* until it reaches the age of education, the very act of entering this world immediately enables it to eat, drink, and select for itself, marking the beginning of its spiritual service as well.

The Rebbe, Rabbi Menachem Mendel Schneerson, *Likutei Sichot*, vol. 2, p. 603

❸ The lamp that burns above a fetus's head within the womb is not a physical flame but a ray of spiritual clarity and vision that the child experiences, which enables it to see from one end of the world to the other. The child's soul can sustain this awareness because, while in the womb, it lacks nothing and is therefore capable of experiencing an awareness of the Torah's complete perfection.

Then, as a child emerges from the womb, an angel touches its mouth and it immediately feels its own hunger, desires to nurse, and loses its awareness of the Torah. This reflects the reality that the sense of material need and lack that we experience in this world makes it difficult to sustain a full awareness of the Torah. Conversely, we are better able to gain clarity when we are content with what we have.

Rabbi Yehudah Loew (Maharal), ***Derashot HaMaharal, Derush leShabbat Teshuvah***

---

❹ Why was it important to teach the fetus material it cannot possibly carry over into life? Why teach what will soon be forgotten?

Rabbi Simla'i is apparently saying that every Jew comes into the world with a natural responsiveness to Torah teaching. Every Jew begins with a share in Torah that was vested in him before his birth, and though he is made to forget it, it is preserved in the deep recesses of his soul, waiting to be awakened by study and a favorable environment. . . . When a Jew studies Torah, he finds it native to his spiritual personality, and he responds to it readily. It is an act of recollecting, recapturing, bringing to the surface what was once learned and forgotten. The Torah did not impose upon the Jews some extraneous matter, foreign to their natures. Rather, Torah study and practice awaken the Jewish memory and we recall that which is inherent in the Jewish soul.

Rabbi Joseph B. Soloveitchik, ***Reflections of the Rav*****, vol. 1, pp. 60–61**

---

❺ The angel's "blow to the mouth" symbolizes the final step that renders the child a complete human being. Human beings are a composite of an intellectual soul and a material body; two qualities that merge in the capacity for speech: We speak with our body but we could not understand the language we use without intellect. As long as a child remains in the womb, its intellectual soul remains apart from the physical body and is able to retain awareness of the entire Torah. Then, at the moment of birth, the soul and the body snap together to form a complete human being, simultaneously creating the potential for speech while causing the soul to forget the Torah.

Rabbi Yehudah Loew (Maharal), ***Gevurot Hashem*****, ch. 28**

---

❻ The angel's strike that "causes [the child] to forget the entire Torah" is a positive act, in the sense that it enables the child to achieve Torah learning through their own exertion. Any achievement we earn through our own efforts is far more precious to us than that which is provided to us or done for us. Therefore, as our sages taught, "A person prefers one measure of their own over nine measures from their fellow." In addition, forgetting the entire Torah provides the child with genuine freedom of choice, through causing the good and the immoral to appear equally appealing.

The Rebbe, Rabbi Menachem Mendel Schneerson, ***Torat Menachem*** **5742, vol. 4, p. 2183;** ***Likutei Sichot*****, vol. 20, p. 108**

---

❼ Our sages inform us that the Divine soul gains knowledge of the entire Torah in utero, and upon birth, is sworn to be righteous and not wicked. It is highly puzzling that the Divine soul must be sworn regarding the possibility of acting wickedly—a possibility that stems not from the Divine soul but from a person's animalistic soul. In fact, all negative traits emerge from the animalistic soul, including anger, pride, lust, frivolity, mockery, vanity, idle talk, and laziness. What purpose is served with an oath that binds the Divine soul on these matters?

Rather, this oath (*shevu'ah*) can be understood as related to "fullness" or "satisfaction" (*sove'a*). It reflects the spiritual truth that each soul is filled by Heaven with the power it requires to fulfill its spiritual duties in alignment with the Torah and *mitzvot*. This oath announces that the Divine soul has been equipped with the strength it will need to overcome the challenges raised by its animalistic soul, so that no obstacle can prevent it from remaining righteous.

Rabbi Shalom Dovber Schneersohn, ***Kuntres Umaayan*****, 14:1**

---

❽ The soul is not sworn to actually consider itself wicked, for the sages warn us, "Do not be wicked in your own eyes" (Avot 2). In fact, if we consider ourselves lowly, we are likely to become depressed or cynical. Rather, the oath adjures the soul to avoid naively thinking that it has overcome all its negative traits and need not exercise self-control.

This oath warns the soul, "Do not be fooled by those who will tell you that you are completely righteous. Always consider yourself 'as if you were wicked,' and bear in mind that negative tendencies still lurk within you—even if you constantly overcome them in actual practice and are therefore able to act like one who is entirely righteous."

Rabbi Shneur Zalman of Liadi, ***Tanya, Likutei Amarim*****, chs. 1, 13**

TEXT 1

The Fire in the Womb

Talmud, Nidah 30b

לְמָה הַוָּלָד דּוֹמֶה בִּמְעֵי אִמּוֹ? לְפִנְקָס שֶׁמְּקֻפָּל, וּמֻנָּח יָדָיו עַל שְׁתֵּי צְדָעָיו, שְׁתֵּי אֲצִילָיו עַל ב' אַרְכֻּבּוֹתָיו, וּב' עֲקֵבָיו עַל ב' עַגְבוֹתָיו, וְרֹאשׁוֹ מוּנָּח לוֹ בֵּין בִּרְכָּיו, וּפִיו סָתוּם וְטַבּוּרוֹ פָּתוּחַ, וְאוֹכֵל מִמָּה שֶׁאִמּוֹ אוֹכֶלֶת וְשׁוֹתֶה מִמָּה שֶׁאִמּוֹ שׁוֹתָה, וְאֵינוֹ מוֹצִיא רְעִי . . .

וְנֵר דָּלוּק לוֹ עַל רֹאשׁוֹ, וְצוֹפֶה וּמַבִּיט מִסּוֹף הָעוֹלָם וְעַד סוֹפוֹ . . .

וּמְלַמְּדִין אוֹתוֹ כָּל הַתּוֹרָה כֻּלָּהּ . . . וְכֵיוָן שֶׁבָּא לַאֲוִיר הָעוֹלָם בָּא מַלְאָךְ וְסְטָרוֹ עַל פִּיו, וּמְשַׁכְּחוֹ כָּל הַתּוֹרָה כֻּלָּהּ . . .

וְאֵינוֹ יוֹצֵא מִשָּׁם עַד שֶׁמַּשְׁבִּיעִין אוֹתוֹ . . . וּמָה הִיא הַשְּׁבוּעָה שֶׁמַּשְׁבִּיעִין אוֹתוֹ? תְּהִי צַדִּיק וְאַל תְּהִי רָשָׁע.

A fetus inside its mother's womb resembles a folded writing tablet: Its two hands rest on its temples, its two elbows rest on its knees, its heels rest against its buttocks, and its head lies between its knees. Its mouth is closed and its navel is open. It eats what its mother eats, drinks what its mother drinks, and produces no excrement. . . .

A lamp burns above its head and it sees from one end of the world to the other. . . .

The fetus is taught the entire Torah. . . . However, as the fetus emerges into the world,

BABYLONIAN TALMUD

A literary work of monumental proportions that draws upon the legal, spiritual, intellectual, ethical, and historical traditions of Judaism. The 37 tractates of the Babylonian Talmud contain the teachings of the Jewish sages from the period after the destruction of the 2nd Temple through the 5th century CE. It has served as the primary vehicle for the transmission of the Oral Law and the education of Jews over the centuries; it is the entry point for all subsequent legal, ethical, and theological Jewish scholarship.

an angel approaches and strikes its mouth, causing it to forget the entire Torah. . . .

The fetus does not emerge before it is made to take an oath. . . . What is the content of the oath? "Be righteous and not wicked."

QUESTION

Does this passage shed any light on whether a fetus should be considered a human life?

WAITING TO BE BORN
Judith Margolis, mixed media collage, gouache, acrylic paint, pastel, colored pencil on paper, 2006, Israel

III. FETAL STATUS IN JEWISH LAW

The above Talmudic passage suggests a degree of philosophical tension. On the one hand, it reveals the presence of a soul associated with the fetus, and indicates a considerable active investment in readying a fetus for life. On the other hand, it betrays the reality that a fetus has yet to gain a full human life, due to its lack of body-soul integration coupled with a lack of any independence.

The following sources will demonstrate that this philosophical tension is also reflected in practical halachic perspectives pertaining to abortion.

Study and analyze the following text, and then proceed to answer the three questions below.

TEXT 2

Cryptic Verses

Exodus 21:22–23

וְכִי יִנָּצוּ אֲנָשִׁים, וְנָגְפוּ אִשָּׁה הָרָה וְיָצְאוּ יְלָדֶיהָ וְלֹא יִהְיֶה אָסוֹן, עָנוֹשׁ יֵעָנֵשׁ . . . וְנָתַן בִּפְלִלִים.

וְאִם אָסוֹן יִהְיֶה, וְנָתַתָּה נֶפֶשׁ תַּחַת נָפֶשׁ.

If men are embroiled in an altercation, and a blow lands on a pregnant woman, and her fetuses emerge and there is no tragedy, the perpetrator must certainly be punished . . . through providing [restitution] in accordance with the judges' orders.

If, however, there is a tragedy, you must provide a life for a life.

EXERCISE 3.2

1. What is the meaning of the phrase: "Her fetuses emerge and there is no tragedy"?

   a. The fetuses and mother survive.

   b. The mother survives but the fetuses die.

2. "The perpetrator must certainly be punished . . . through providing [restitution]." What is the basis for this restitution?

   a. Provoking a premature but healthy birth.

   b. Causing the death of the fetuses.

3. What is the meaning of the phrase, "If there is a tragedy, you must provide a life for a life"?

   a. If the fetuses die, the assailant receives the death penalty.

   b. If the mother dies, the assailant receives the death penalty.

TEXT 3

Saving a Fetus on Shabbat

Talmud, Arachin 7a

הָאִשָּׁה שֶׁיָּשְׁבָה עַל הַמַּשְׁבֵּר וּמֵתָה בְּשַׁבָּת,
מְבִיאִין סַכִּין וּמְקָרְעִים אֶת כְּרֵסָהּ וּמוֹצִיאִין אֶת הַוָּלָד.

פְּשִׁיטָא, מַאי עָבִיד? מְחַתֵּךְ בְּבָשָׂר הוּא!

אָמַר רַבָּה: לֹא נִצְרְכָה, לְהָבִיא סַכִּין דֶּרֶךְ רְשׁוּת הָרַבִּים.

If, on Shabbat, a woman sitting on a birthstool dies [before she was able to deliver her child], they should fetch a knife and cut open her womb to extract the child.

[The Talmud objects:] But that statement is obvious—there is no prohibition against cutting flesh on Shabbat!

Rabah responded, "The statement is necessary to permit the fetching of the knife by way of a public thoroughfare [which is prohibited on Shabbat]."

Jewish medical ethicist **Rabbi Edward Reichman, M.D.** discusses abortion: **myjli.com/decisions**

TEXT 4

The Mother over the Fetus

Mishnah, Ohalot 7:6

הָאִשָּׁה שֶׁהִיא מַקְשָׁה לֵלֵד, מְחַתְּכִין אֶת הַוָּלָד בְּמֵעֶיהָ
וּמוֹצִיאִין אוֹתוֹ אֵבָרִים אֵבָרִים, מִפְּנֵי שֶׁחַיֶּיהָ קוֹדְמִין לְחַיָּיו.

If a woman experiences [life-threatening] difficulties during labor, we cut the fetus in her womb and extract it limb by limb, because her life takes precedence over the fetus's life.

MISHNAH

The first authoritative work of Jewish law that was codified in writing. The Mishnah contains the oral traditions that were passed down from teacher to student; it supplements, clarifies, and systematizes the commandments of the Torah. Due to the continual persecution of the Jewish people, it became increasingly difficult to guarantee that these traditions would not be forgotten. Rabbi Yehudah Hanasi therefore redacted the Mishnah at the end of the 2nd century. It serves as the foundation for the Talmud.

Postpartum scene from the *Harrison Miscellany*, a collection of illustrations connected with the Book of Genesis, relating to marriage, interspersed with biblical verses and sayings. Corfu, first half of 18th century (Braginsky Collection)

The following two classic texts explain the logic of the law in the above Mishnah. Compare them carefully and identify the differences between them.

TEXT 5

Not Yet a Life

Rashi, Sanhedrin 72b

הַחַיָּה פּוֹשֶׁטֶת יָדָהּ וְחוֹתַכְתּוֹ וּמוֹצִיאָתוֹ לְאֵבָרִים. דְּכָל זְמַן שֶׁלֹּא יָצָא לַאֲוִיר הָעוֹלָם לָאו נֶפֶשׁ הוּא, וְנִתַּן לְהוֹרְגוֹ וּלְהַצִּיל אֶת אִמּוֹ.

A midwife reaches [into the womb] with her hand to dismember the fetus and extract it limb by limb. For as long as a fetus has not emerged into the world, it is not a life. It is therefore permitted to kill it for the sake of saving the mother's life.

RABBI SHLOMO YITZCHAKI (RASHI) 1040–1105

Most noted biblical and Talmudic commentator. Born in Troyes, France, Rashi studied in the famed *yeshivot* of Mainz and Worms. His commentaries on the Pentateuch and the Talmud, which focus on the straightforward meaning of the text, appear in virtually every edition of the Talmud and Bible.

Title page from the Jewish births diary/register of a midwife, Roza, wife of Leyzer ben Moses Judah, in Yiddish (L.) and Hebrew (R), begun in 1794, Groningen, Holland (Posen Digital Library of Jewish Culture and Civilization)

TEXT 6

Fetal Pursuit

Maimonides, *Mishneh Torah,*
Laws of the Murderer and Preserving Life 1:9

הֲרֵי זוֹ מִצְוַת לֹא תַעֲשֶׂה שֶׁלֹּא לָחוּס עַל נֶפֶשׁ הָרוֹדֵף. לְפִיכָךְ הוֹרוּ חֲכָמִים שֶׁהָעֻבָּרָה שֶׁהִיא מַקְשָׁה לֵילֵד, מֻתָּר לַחְתֹּךְ הָעֻבָּר בְּמֵעֶיהָ, בֵּין בְּסַם בֵּין בְּיָד, מִפְּנֵי שֶׁהוּא כְּרוֹדֵף אַחֲרֶיהָ לְהָרְגָהּ.

We are commanded to not take pity on the life of a *rodef*, a murderous pursuer, [if that is necessary to rescue the intended victim].

On this basis, our sages ruled that if a woman experiences [life-threatening] complications during labor, it is permitted to abort the fetus in her womb, with drugs or with an instrument. For the fetus is considered a form of *rodef* against its mother.

RABBI MOSHE BEN MAIMON (MAIMONIDES, RAMBAM) 1135–1204

Halachist, philosopher, author, and physician. Maimonides was born in Córdoba, Spain. After the conquest of Córdoba by the Almohads, he fled Spain and eventually settled in Cairo, Egypt. There, he became the leader of the Jewish community and served as court physician to the vizier of Egypt. He is most noted for authoring the *Mishneh Torah*, an encyclopedic arrangement of Jewish law; and for his philosophical work, *Guide for the Perplexed*. His rulings on Jewish law are integral to the formation of Halachic consensus.

MAIMONIDES
Arthur Szyk (1894 [Lodz, Poland]–1951 [New Caanan, Conn., via France and U.K.]), 20th-century watercolor and gouache on paper, in the medieval-Renaissance style Szyk sometimes emulated, 1950 (Yeshiva University Museum, New York, N.Y.)

EXERCISE 3.3

	DIFFERENCE 1	DIFFERENCE 2
RASHI		
MAIMONIDES		

TEXT 7

Surrender to Divine Will

Rabbi Moshe Feinstein, *Igrot Moshe, Choshen Mishpat* 2:69–71

אִיכָּא אִסּוּר רְצִיחָה מִ"לֹא תִּרְצָח" גַם עַל עֻבָּר, וְרַק שֶׁפָּטוּר הַהוֹרְגוֹ מִמִּיתָה . . . וְרַק לְהַצָּלַת אִמּוֹ שֶׁלֹּא תָּמוּת בְּלֵדָתוֹ הוּא הַהֶתֵּר . . .

אַף הַוְּלָדוֹת שֶׁלְּפִי דַּעַת הָרוֹפְאִים הֵם כָּאֵלּוּ שֶׁלֹּא יִחְיוּ שָׁנִים רַבּוֹת, כְּהָא דְנוֹלָדִים אֵיזֶה יְלָדִים בְּמַחֲלָה הַנִּקְרֵאת תַּיי סַקְס, אֲפִלּוּ כְּשֶׁנּוֹדַע עַל יְדֵי הַבְּדִיקוֹת בָּעֻבָּר שֶׁנִּתְחַדֵּשׁ עַתָּה שֶׁהַוָּלָד יִהְיֶה וְלַד כָּזֶה, אָסוּר. כֵּיוָן דִלְהָאֵם לֵיכָּא סַכָּנָה, וְאֵינוֹ רוֹדֵף, אֵין לְהַתִּיר אֲפִלּוּ שֶׁהַצַּעַר יִהְיֶה גָדוֹל . . .

וּבִכְלָל יֵשׁ לֵדַע כִּי הַכֹּל הוּא מִשָּׁמַיִם . . . צָרִיךְ לְקַבֵּל בְּאַהֲבָה כָּל מָה שֶׁעוֹשֶׂה ה' יִתְבָּרַךְ:

RABBI MOSHE FEINSTEIN 1895–1986

Leading Halachic authority of the 20th century. Rabbi Feinstein was appointed rabbi of Luban, Belarus, in 1921. He immigrated to the U.S. in 1937 and became the dean of Metivta Tiferet Yerushalayim in New York. Rabbi Feinstein's Halachic decisions have been published in a multivolume collection entitled *Igrot Moshe*.

Abortion is forbidden as an act of murder. The only distinction between abortion and the murder of an already-born human is that one is not liable to receive the death penalty for killing a fetus. . . . The only instance in which abortion can be permitted is when it is necessary in order to save the life of the fetus's mother. . . .

This applies even to a fetus that the doctors predict will only be able to survive for a few years, such as children born with Tay-Sachs disease. Even if the diagnostic tests that have recently been developed determine that the child will be born with this disease, it is forbidden to abort. Although this will cause great pain to the parents, nevertheless, since the mother's life is not endangered by the fetus, abortion cannot be permitted. . . .

We must acknowledge that G-d is directly in charge of all events . . . and we need to accept everything He does with love.

The overturning of Roe v. Wade: a Jewish perspective: **myjli.com/decisions**

TEXT 8

Acute Circumstances

Rabbi Eliezer Yehudah Waldenberg, *Tzitz Eliezer* 13:102

הַשְּׁאֵלָה הִיא אוֹדוֹת הַפְסָקַת הֵרָיוֹן בִּגְלַל הַמַּחֲלָה הַנִּקְרֵאת תַּיי סַקְס, אֲשֶׁר אַבְחָנָתָהּ מִתְגַּלֵּית עוֹד בְּשְׁלַבֵּי הַהֵרָיוֹן . . . הַאִם לִרְאוֹת בְּמַחֲלָה זוֹ, אֲשֶׁר תּוֹצְאוֹתָהּ כֹּה חֲמוּרוֹת וְכֹה וַדָּאִיּוֹת, מַסְפִּיק חָמוּר בִּכְדֵי לְאַפְשֵׁר הַפְסָקַת הֵרָיוֹן . . .

אַחֲרֵי הָעִיּוּן בַּדָּבָר בְּכֹבֶד רֹאשׁ בְּכָל צְדָדֵי הַנְּתוּנִים שֶׁבַּבְּעָיָה הָאֲמוּרָה, נִרְאֶה לְפִי עֲנִיּוּת דַעְתִּי עַל יְסוֹד הַבֵּרוּרִים הַנִּרְחָבִים שֶׁכָּתַבְתִּי בִּדְבַר הַפְסָקַת הֵרָיוֹן בְּסִפְרִי, שְׁאֵלוֹת וּתְשׁוּבוֹת צִיץ אֱלִיעֶזֶר חֵלֶק ט, סִימָן נא שַׁעַר ג עַל שְׁלֹשֶׁת פְּרָקָיו הָאֲרֻכִּים, כִּי שֶׁבַּמִּקְרֶה הַמְיֻחָד הַזֶּה, אֲשֶׁר תּוֹצָאוֹת כֹּה חֲמוּרוֹת בִּכְנָפָיו עִם הַמְשָׁכַת הַהֵרָיוֹן וְהַלֵּדָה, אֶפְשָׁר לְהַתִּיר הַפְסָקַת הֵרָיוֹן עַד שִׁבְעָה חֳדָשִׁים . . .

מִשִּׁבְעָה חֳדָשִׁים וָהָלְאָה הַדָּבָר כְּבָר יוֹתֵר חָמוּר . . . כֵּיוָן שֶׁבִּמְלֹאת ז' חֳדָשִׁים בָּא כְּבָר הַוָּלָד בְּהַרְבֵּה מִקְרִים לִידֵי גְּמְרוֹ.

You inquired about the permissibility of abortion in a case of Tay-Sachs disease, which can be diagnosed during pregnancy. . . . The consequences of this disease are extremely severe and untreatable, and you asked whether this constitutes sufficient grounds to permit an abortion. . . .

After carefully considering all aspects of this issue, my conclusion is that in this unique case, where

RABBI ELIEZER YEHUDAH WALDENBERG
1915–2006

Noted Halachic authority. Rabbi Waldenberg served as judge on the Supreme Rabbinical Court in Jerusalem and was known as an eminent authority on Jewish medical ethics and Jewish law. He published his Halachic responsa, *Tzitz Eliezer*, which is viewed as one of the great achievements of Halachic scholarship of the 20th century. He served as rabbi for the Shaare Zedek Medical Center in Jerusalem.

Renowned Jewish legal authority **Rabbi Hershel Schachter** provides insight on abortion and Halachah: **myjli.com/decisions**

the consequences of continuing the pregnancy and bringing the child to term are so severe, it is possible to permit an abortion before the fetus reaches seven months. I base this conclusion on the lengthy halachic analysis of the status of abortion that I published in *Tzitz Eliezer* 9:51 [which presents the conclusion that abortion does not constitute an act of murder]. . . .

After seven months, abortion is a far weightier decision . . . because at that stage, the fetus typically attains a state of viability.

RIVKA EXPECTING
Shoshannah Brombacher, pastel and India ink drawing, 2007, Brooklyn. At the bottom are the words from Genesis 25:23, "Two nations are in your womb."

TEXT 9

Early Fluidity

Talmud, Yevamot 69b

בַּת כֹּהֵן שֶׁנִּשֵּׂאת לְיִשְׂרָאֵל וָמֵת,
טוֹבֶלֶת וְאוֹכֶלֶת בִּתְרוּמָה לָעֶרֶב.

אָמַר רַב חִסְדָּא: טוֹבֶלֶת וְאוֹכֶלֶת עַד אַרְבָּעִים, דְּאִי לֹא מִעַבְּרָא,
הָא לֹא מִעַבְּרָא. וְאִי מִעַבְּרָא, עַד אַרְבָּעִים מַיָּא בְּעַלְמָא הִיא.

If a daughter of a *Kohen* married a non-*Kohen* and he died [on the wedding night], she may immerse in the *mikveh* and eat *terumah* that evening.

[Why are we not concerned that she may be pregnant?] Rav Chisda said, "She may eat *terumah* until forty days [from her marriage] because if she is not pregnant, there is no disqualifying factor, and if she is pregnant, until forty days have elapsed the embryo is mere fluid."

JERUSALEM
Tzvi Raphaeli (1924 [Egypt]–2005 [Israel]), oil on canvas, mid-20th-century, Israel (Leviim Art Gallery, Brooklyn, NY)

IV. CONCLUSION

After surveying the varying opinions within Jewish law regarding abortion, it is possible to return to the opening case study and attempt to resolve it.

TEXT 10

A Mother's Choice

Rabbi Moshe Sternbuch, *Teshuvot Vehanhagot* 2:777

כְּשֶׁרוֹפְאִים אֵין יְכוֹלִים לְהַחְלִיט עַל מִדַּת הַסַּכָּנָה, וְכַנִּרְאֶה שֶׁהַסָּפֵק שָׁקוּל, וּבְוַדַּאי אֵין הַסַּכָּנָה קְרוֹבָה, אָנוּ מוֹרִים לְהַתִּיר הַהַפָּלָה.

אֲבָל אִם הָאִשָּׁה מִתְעַקֶּשֶׁת שֶׁאֵין רְצוֹנָהּ בְּכָךְ, וַאֲפִלּוּ בְּזֶה רְצוֹנָהּ לִסְמֹךְ עַל רַחֲמֵי ה' וַחֲסָדָיו, כֵּיוָן שֶׁהָאִסּוּר רְצִיחָה וְהַהֶתֵּר לָרַמְבַּ"ם רַק מִדִּין רוֹדֵף דְּמַיְרִי רַק בְּוַדַּאי, לֹא נוּכַל לְמוֹנְעָהּ, וִיכוֹלָה אַף בְּזֶה לִסְמֹךְ עַל רַחֲמֵי ה' וַחֲסָדָיו.

כְּשֶׁלְּדַעַת הָרוֹפְאִים הַסַּכָּנָה קְרוֹבָה, וְהַסִּכּוּיִים לִחְיוֹת מוּעָטִים, אָסוּר לָהּ לִסְמֹךְ לְהָקֵל וּלְהַכְנִיס עַצְמָהּ לַחֲשַׁשׁ סַכָּנָה מַמָּשׁ. שֶׁכְּהַאי גַּוְנָא דּוֹחִין נֶפֶשׁ עֻבָּר מִפְּנֵי אַחֵר, וְאָנוּ מוֹרִים לָהּ לְהַפִּיל הַוָּלָד דַּוְקָא, וְלֹא לְהִסְתַּכֵּן.

When the doctors are not clear about the degree of danger the pregnancy poses to the mother, and the risk appears to be at a level of 50 percent or less, we rule that the abortion is allowed.

RABBI MOSHE STERNBUCH 1926–

Halachic authority. Born in London, Rabbi Moshe Sternbuch was educated in *yeshivot* in England and Israel. He served as a rabbi in Johannesburg, South Africa, before returning to Israel, where he serves as the chief judge of the highly regarded rabbinic court of the Edah Hacharedit in Jerusalem and the head of a yeshiva in Beit Shemesh. A prolific author, Rabbi Sternbuch is best known for his 7-volume series titled *Teshuvot Vehanhagot*, a collection of his Halachic responsa.

Abortion is not an option, unless . . . **Rabbi Manis Friedman**, the most popular rabbi on YouTube, offers insight: **myjli.com/decisions**

However, if the mother insists that she does not want to proceed with an abortion and instead wishes to rely on G-d's mercy and kindness, we cannot stand in her way—she may choose such an approach. For there is room to argue that Maimonides would only permit abortion when a fetus is *clearly* a *rodef* that threatens its mother's life. Although we do not follow that position, nevertheless, if a mother insists on acting in accordance with this position, we cannot prevent her; she may choose to rely on G-d's mercy and kindness.

By contrast, when the doctors state that the danger is *clear*, and the mother's chances of survival are minimal, it is then forbidden for the mother to choose to be lenient about her own life and place herself in such serious danger. In such a scenario, we unequivocally instruct her that she is halachically obligated to undergo an abortion and that she may not endanger herself.

Halachic Responsa Map

Throughout the ages, halachic authorities have grappled with distressing dilemmas caused by medical complications. Many of these dilemmas have been captured for posterity in written rabbinical responses to real-life inquiries. As a sample, we present a question addressed to contemporary halachic authority Rabbi Yitzchak Zilberstein in the summer of 1986, followed by a digest of the key points of his response. The original full question and responsa is published in *Shiurei Torah Lerofim*, vol. 4, responsa 245.

Biographical Sketch

Rabbi Yitzchak Zilberstein was born in Poland in 1934, and was raised in Israel, where he studied at Jerusalem and Bnei Brak yeshivot. He serves as the rabbi of Bnei Brak's Ramat Elchanan neighborhood and is the author of several works on Jewish law and ethics. He specializes in the field of Jewish medical ethics, and his responsa in this field are collected in five volumes, under the title *Shiurei Torah Lerofim*.

The Inquiry

A QUESTION OF MULTI-FETAL REDUCTION

It is common to prescribe fertility drugs that induce ovulation to women suffering from infertility. This treatment often causes a multi-fetal pregnancy—there has even been a case of septuplets. Such pregnancies involve considerable complications for the mother and fetuses. The primary problem in these situations is premature birth, which because of pulmonary immaturity, endangers the lives of the newborns. The higher the number of fetuses, the earlier their birth will be, and the earlier their birth, the more serious the condition.

Recently, several medical centers have tried to solve this problem by performing multi-fetal pregnancy reductions in order to increase the chances of survival for the remaining fetuses.

I was consulted about a case of a thirty-four-year-old woman who is pregnant for the first time after hormone therapy. She is in the first trimester and is pregnant with seven fetuses. The physician has suggested fetal reduction.

My question is twofold:

1. **Is it advisable, permitted, or forbidden to perform this procedure?**
2. **If permitted, how many fetuses should be reduced?**

With respect and appreciation,

Pinchas Osher, M.D.
Hadassah Medical Center, Jerusalem

1. The Concept of a *Rodef*

Maimonides writes: "We are commanded to not take pity on the life of a *rodef*, a murderous pursuer, [if that is necessary to rescue the intended victim]. On this basis, our sages ruled that if a woman experiences [life-threatening] complications during labor, it is permitted to abort the fetus in her womb, with drugs or with an instrument. For the fetus is considered a form of *rodef* against its mother" (*Mishneh Torah*, Laws of the Murderer and Preserving Life 1:9).

In light of this decision, if the multi-fetal pregnancy reaches the point that it endangers the mother's life, the fetuses gain the status of a *rodef*, and it becomes permitted to abort one or more to ensure her survival.

2. Who Endangers Whom?

However, the case in question is less clear-cut than the above. In the present scenario, the mother's life is not in jeopardy and the fetuses only pose a danger to each other. If none are aborted, none will survive. Each poses an existential threat to the others, so we can view all the fetuses as both deadly pursuers as well as pursued victims. There is no way to single out any of them as the pursuers of the others, so perhaps it is best to take no action.

3. Sacrificing One to Save Many?

The Talmud discusses a case in which a hostile army orders a group of Jews to hand over one specific member of their group to be killed—failing which, the entire group will be put to death. Is the group permitted to surrender the wanted individual to save the rest? Some authorities—

4. Unviable Lives: A New Equation

The above-stated opinions of Rashi and Maimonides concern the lives of fully developed, independently living individuals who, if nature were permitted to run its course, would have long lives ahead of them. By contrast, the unborn fetuses are naturally doomed, and will never reach the state of independent life. It can be argued that in our case both Rashi and Maimonides would agree that the fetuses do not have proper life status, and fetal reduction would therefore be considered an act of rescuing the remaining fetuses, rather than an act of killing some of them.

such as **Rabbi Shlomo Yitzchaki** (Rashi) in his commentary on the Talmud (*Sanhedrin* 72b)—maintain that it is forbidden to hand over the wanted individual to save the group, if the wanted person has any survival prospects. However, if refusing to hand over the wanted person will certainly result in death for the entire group *including* the wanted individual, it is permissible to hand over the wanted person, because either way this person has no chance of survival.

Others reject this distinction. **Maimonides** rules that it is never acceptable to send one person to their death to save others, even when it is clear that everyone, including the wanted person, will otherwise perish (*Mishneh Torah*, Laws of the Foundations of the Torah 5:5; also see *Kesef Mishneh*, ad loc.).

In the case of fetal reduction, it can be argued that Rashi would allow for some of the fetuses to be aborted, because otherwise all of them will be doomed. Maimonides, however, would forbid such a course of action.

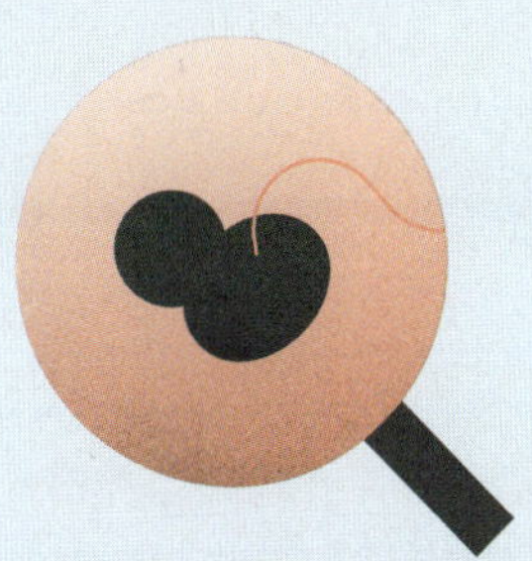

5. The Hardest Choice

If we are correct in our assumption that fetal reduction is ethical in this particular scenario, we must still address the second question: How many fetuses should be reduced? Should we prioritize the survival chances of those who remain and reduce more, or should we try to deliver as many as possible into the world?

Each case must be considered individually. Medical experts must be consulted, and they would need to determine, as objectively as possible, the number of fetuses that must be removed for the remaining fetuses to survive. We must strive to find the middle path between the two priorities and pass judgment in trembling and fear, and in prayer before G-d, for we sit in judgment over human lives.

KEY POINTS

1 According to the Talmud, a human fetus possesses a soul. In utero, while the fetus physically develops and grows, its soul, too, spiritually develops and is fortified with the spiritual powers necessary for it to lead a productive spiritual life.

2 G-d perceives every person's uniqueness and the distinct contribution that each person will bring to the world. He therefore invests so much in each fetus, so that it is equipped to succeed in the commission of its unique mission.

3 There is a halachic consensus that abortion is a very grave matter, and usually forbidden by Jewish law.

4 However, there is debate regarding the degree of the prohibition's severity. Some halachic authorities consider abortion akin to murder and only allow it when the pregnancy is endangering the mother's life. However, other halachic authorities maintain that abortion is not akin to murder, and they allow it in certain very acute circumstances.

LESSON 4

A BODY'S DIGNITY

Might autopsy violate the dignity of the human body? Learn the Jewish view on the respect due the deceased and how the sanctity of human life continues after death.

THE JEWISH CEMETERY OF PRAGUE
Shoshannah Brombacher, oil on canvas, 1993, Brooklyn

I. INTRODUCTION

When human life ends, the soul departs and a body remains behind. In this lesson, we will explore the perspective of Jewish thought and law on the proper handling of human remains, and its ramifications for autopsies, anatomical education, and burial.

CASE STUDY

Alexis Allison, "Cadavers Help Students Prepare for Professions in Medicine. But Some Are Donated without Consent," April 3, 2022, fortworthreport.org

In the anatomy lab at The University of North Texas Health Science Center at Fort Worth, medical students interact with what some consider their very first patients: dead people who, more often than not, chose to donate their bodies to science through the school's Willed Body Program. They provide the repetition that leads to confidence for students who will one day treat living patients.

But about one in four cadavers belong to those the county calls "unclaimed": people whose families couldn't afford or chose not to provide funeral services, or those whose next of kin couldn't be found. Not only has the program saved Tarrant County hundreds of thousands of dollars in its first three years alone, it's provided a more diverse donor pool from which students can learn. . . .

Texas law requires each county's commissioners' court to care for the bodies of people who can't afford funeral arrangements. An attorney general opinion in 2000 noted the language allows the county to donate the body to a medical facility.

Before contracting with the Health Science Center, Tarrant County offered burials or cremations at no cost to the person's family, according to Lisa Martin, director of the Tarrant County Department of Human Services. The expenses cost the county roughly half a million each year.

After the contract went into effect, those expenses plummeted. The county mostly stopped offering burials—the most costly option—though exceptions for unidentified bodies, veterans and people with certain religious beliefs remain. . . .

Eli Shupe was volunteering at a hospice in Arlington in late 2021 when she learned about the Health Science Center's contract with Tarrant County. A chaplain with whom she made weekly rounds mentioned one patient wouldn't survive much longer.

"After he died, he'd 'go to the med school,'" Shupe said. "And I asked what that meant. . . . That's how I learned that this is what happens when you die with no assets."

Shupe, a recent transplant to Texas, had earned a Ph.D. in philosophy and was well-steeped in the world of donation—in

Who defines life and death? **Rabbi Manis Friedman**, the most popular rabbi on YouTube, offers insight: **myjli.com/decisions**

2018, she donated one of her kidneys. She now teaches bioethics at UT-Arlington.

Her concerns with the program were both philosophical and practical. She mulled over consent, or lack thereof. People have a right to make decisions about their bodies while they're alive, she said. "A deep philosophical question to ask is, 'Does that right persist after we die?'"

For Shupe, the answer is yes. In December, she published a column in the Dallas Morning News critiquing the program. She didn't want to solely offer criticism, so she signed up to, one day, donate her body to the Health Science Center's program. The consent forms abounded.

"If they think it's important for me to sign all of those consents, clearly, they think the fact that I'm making this unpressured, autonomous decision to give my body to them is important," she said. "So, why do they not need those consents for someone who just happened to have nothing when they died?" . . .

Alternatives exist. In 2016, New York banned the use of unclaimed bodies as cadavers. The state's medical schools said they would fill any gaps by expanding their programs for private donations. Closer to home, Bexar County provides a "simple, respectful and dignified service" for people who can't afford them. Furthermore, some medical schools around the country have decided to avoid cadavers altogether in favor of virtual anatomy tools.

At a minimum, Shupe said, programs like the one at the Health Science Center can make informed decisions about what a person with no assets or next of kin likely would have wanted. For example, the majority of Americans now prefer cremation to burial. But, she said, a "vanishingly small number" of people choose to donate their whole bodies—so the more ethical path is to err on the side of caution.

"This is uncomfortably close to grave-robbing," she said. "That's how it seems to me. They just don't go in the ground first." . . .

Students aren't necessarily aware that the cadavers in the anatomy lab may be unclaimed. [Fourth-year medical student Russell Vo said that] as long as the program diligently tried to contact next of kin, and as long as the program approached the bodies with respect, he was OK with it.

"It's a very honorable means," he said, "just because it goes to a good cause to foster the education of medical professionals as a whole." . . .

"These are lifesaving things that (the students are) learning and doing," [Claudia Yellott of the Health Science Center] said. "Not just lifesaving, but quality of life, to be able to restore that quality of life for others, to be able to get something like that out of a tragic loss—where nobody's wanting to be involved—for me is a good thing."

EXERCISE 4.1

Provide arguments for and against the use of unclaimed bodies for anatomical education.

ARGUMENTS FOR	ARGUMENTS AGAINST

II. DEFINING DESECRATION

The use of cadavers in medical research is standard fare. However, the practice raises two distinct halachic issues: the dissection of the corpse, and the failure to promptly bury the dead. Today's lesson continues with an exploration of the viewpoint of Jewish law on the standard autopsy—the performance of a postmortem dissection to study disease or to determine the cause of death.

TEXT 1

Respecting Remains

Talmud, Berachot 18a

הַמּוֹלִיךְ עֲצָמוֹת מִמָּקוֹם לְמָקוֹם, הֲרֵי זֶה לֹא יִתְּנֵם בְּדִסְקַיָּא וְיִתְּנֵם עַל גַּבֵּי חֲמוֹר וְיִרְכַּב עֲלֵיהֶם, מִפְּנֵי שֶׁנּוֹהֵג בָּהֶם מִנְהַג בִּזָּיוֹן.

One who transports human bones on a donkey may not place them in a leather saddlebag and ride on top of them, for by doing so, one treats them disrespectfully.

BABYLONIAN TALMUD

A literary work of monumental proportions that draws upon the legal, spiritual, intellectual, ethical, and historical traditions of Judaism. The 37 tractates of the Babylonian Talmud contain the teachings of the Jewish sages from the period after the destruction of the 2nd Temple through the 5th century CE. It has served as the primary vehicle for the transmission of the Oral Law and the education of Jews over the centuries; it is the entry point for all subsequent legal, ethical, and theological Jewish scholarship.

QUESTION

What might be the rationale against acting "disrespectfully" toward human remains?

TEXT 2

Dissecting Emergency

Rabbi Yaakov Ettlinger, *Binyan Tziyon* 170

נִשְׁאַלְתִּי: חוֹלֶה אֶחָד נֶחְלָה בְּחֹלִי נִפְלָא, וְעָסְקוּ הָרוֹפְאִים בִּרְפוּאָתוֹ לְלֹא הוֹעִיל, כִּי מֵת בְּחָלְיוֹ. וְיֵשׁ שָׁם עוֹד חוֹלֶה שֶׁנֶּחְלָה בְּחֹלִי כָּזֶה, וְרָצוּ הָרוֹפְאִים לִפְתֹּחַ אֶת הַמֵּת לִרְאוֹת עִנְיַן הַחֹלִי, לְמַעַן מְצֹא תְּרוּפָה לַאֲשֶׁר עוֹד בַּחַיִּים.

אִם מֻתָּר לַעֲשׂוֹת כֵּן לְנַוֵּל הַמֵּת אוֹ לֹא?

I was consulted regarding the case of a patient who was ill with a unique disease. The doctors treated him, but to no avail—he died of his illness. Another patient suffered from the same illness, and the doctors sought to dissect the body of the deceased person to understand the disease and possibly find a cure for the patient who was still alive.

Under such circumstances, is it permissible to desecrate the dead?

RABBI YAAKOV ETTLINGER
1798–1871

German Halachic authority. Rabbi Ettlinger was born in Karlsruhe, Germany. In 1836, he became chief rabbi of Altona, where he remained until his death. He was one of the most prominent representatives of German Orthodoxy, which stood for the union of secular learning with adherence to traditional Judaism. He authored *Aruch Lener,* a popular commentary on the Talmud. Among his disciples was Rabbi Shimshon Raphael Hirsch.

TEXT 3

Stealing in Danger

Rabbi Yaakov ben Asher, *Arbaah Turim, Choshen Mishpat* 359

וַאֲפִלוּ אִם הוּא בְּסַכָּנַת מָוֶת וּבָא לִגְזֹל אֶת חֲבֵרוֹ וּלְהַצִּיל אֶת נַפְשׁוֹ, אָסוּר לוֹ לִגְזֹל אִם לֹא עַל דַעַת לְשַׁלֵם. דְוַדַאי אֵין לְךָ דָבָר הָעוֹמֵד בִּפְנֵי פִּקוּחַ נֶפֶשׁ, לְכָךְ הוּא רַשַׁאי לִטְלוֹ וּלְהַצִּיל נַפְשׁוֹ, אֲבָל לֹא יִקָחֵנוּ אֶלָא עַל דַעַת לְשַׁלֵם.

Nothing stands in the way of saving a life. Nevertheless, if people are in mortal danger and must steal from their fellows in order to save their lives, it is forbidden for them to do so without intention to repay.

RABBI YAAKOV BEN ASHER (*TUR*, BAAL HATURIM) C. 1269–C. 1343

Halachic authority and codifier. Rabbi Yaakov was born in Germany and moved to Toledo, Spain, with his father, the noted Halachist Rabbi Asher, to escape persecution. He wrote *Arbaah Turim* ("*Tur*"), an ingeniously organized and highly influential code of Jewish law. He is considered one of the greatest authorities on Halachah.

QUESTION

What might be the rationale for insisting on an intention to reimburse when theft is critical to saving a life?

Rabbi YY Jacobson discusses the importance of upholding the dignity of the human body: **myjli.com/decisions**

TEXT 4

Unpayable Debt

Rabbi Yaakov Ettlinger, *Binyan Tziyon* 170

הֲרֵי בְּפֵרוּשׁ דְאָסוּר לִגְזֹל אֲפִלוּ לְהַצִיל נֶפֶשׁ אִם לֹא עַל מְנַת לְשַׁלֵם . . . וּלְפִי זֶה, בְּנִדוֹן זֶה דְלֹא שַׁיָךְ שֶׁיְשַׁלֵם לְבַסוֹף, דְאִי אֶפְשָׁר לְשַׁלֵם לַמֵת אֶת בִּזְיוֹנוֹ . . . אָסוּר לְהַצִיל נֶפֶשׁ בְּבִזְיוֹן אַחֵר.

It is stated explicitly that it is forbidden to steal to save a life if one has no intention to repay. . . . In the present case, it is impossible to repay, inasmuch as one cannot compensate the deceased for having been desecrated. It is therefore forbidden to save a life through the desecration of the deceased.

CEMETERY GATES
Marc Chagall, painting, 1917. The words across the gates are from Ezekiel 37:12, predicting the messianic Redemption's fulfillment of the prophecy of the Resurrection of the Dead. (Musée d'Art et d'Histoire du Judaïsme, Paris, France)

EXERCISE 4.2

When would Rabbi Ettlinger consider autopsy a forbidden desecration of a corpse?

	ARGUMENTS FOR	ARGUMENTS AGAINST
THE DECEASED CONSENTED		
THE DECEASED DID NOT CONSENT		

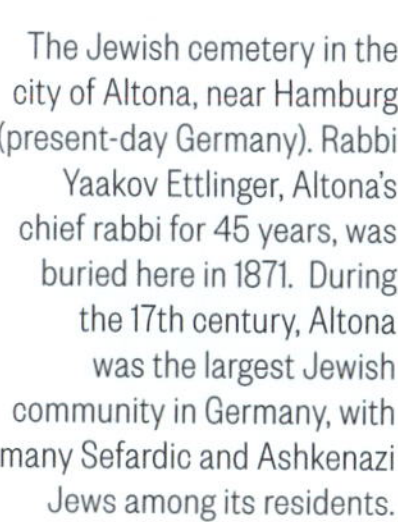

The Jewish cemetery in the city of Altona, near Hamburg (present-day Germany). Rabbi Yaakov Ettlinger, Altona's chief rabbi for 45 years, was buried here in 1871. During the 17th century, Altona was the largest Jewish community in Germany, with many Sefardic and Ashkenazi Jews among its residents.

TEXT 5

Immediate Rescue

Rabbi Yechezkel Landau, *Noda BiYehudah, Tinyana, Yoreh De'ah* 210

זֶה הוּא דִין עָרוּךְ וּמְפֹרָשׁ שֶׁאֲפִלוּ סָפֵק דוֹחֶה שַׁבָּת הַחֲמוּרָה . . .

וְאָמְנָם כָּל זֶה בְּיֵשׁ סְפֵק סַכָּנַת נְפָשׁוֹת לְפָנֵינוּ, כְּגוֹן חוֹלֶה אוֹ נְפִילַת הַגַל . . . אֲבָל בְּנִדוֹן דִידַן, אֵין כָּאן שׁוּם חוֹלֶה הַצָּרִיךְ לְזֶה, רַק שֶׁרוֹצִים לִלְמֹד חָכְמָה זוּ אוּלַי יִזְדַמֵן חוֹלֶה שֶׁיִהְיֶה צָרִיךְ לָזֶה. וַדַאי דְלֹא דָחִינַן מִשׁוּם חֲשָׁשָׁא קַלָה זוּ שׁוּם אִסוּר . . .

שֶׁאִם אַתָּה קוֹרֵא לַחֲשָׁשָׁא זוּ סְפֵק נְפָשׁוֹת, אִם כֵּן יִהְיֶה כָּל מְלֶאכֶת הָרְפוּאוֹת - שְׁחִיקַת וּבִשׁוּל סַמָנִים וַהֲכָנַת כְּלֵי אִזְמֵל לְהַקָזָה - מֻתָּר בְּשַׁבָּת, שֶׁמָא יִזְדַמֵן הַיוֹם אוֹ בַּלַיְלָה חוֹלֶה, שֶׁיִהְיֶה צֹרֶךְ לָזֶה . . .

וְאִם אָנוּ חַס וְשָׁלוֹם מְקִלִים בְּדָבָר זֶה, אִם כֵּן יְנַתְּחוּ כָּל הַמֵתִים כְּדֵי לִלְמֹד סִדוּר הָאֵבָרִים הַפְּנִימִיִים וּמַהוּתָן, כְּדֵי שֶׁיֵדְעוּ לַעֲשׂוֹת רְפוּאוֹת לְהַחַיִים.

It is a clearly established law that we must override the Shabbat laws in our attempt to save a life, even if the chance of success is doubtful. . . .

However, this is true only if there is a present threat to life before us, as in the case of an ill person or a collapsed building. . . . But in this case, there is no current patient who would

RABBI YECHEZKEL LANDAU (*NODA BIYEHUDAH*) 1713–1793

Halachist. Rabbi Landau was born in Poland. In 1755, he assumed the rabbinate of Prague and all of Bohemia. An influential authority on Halachah, he responded to queries from all over Europe, most of which have been collected and published in *Responsa Noda BiYehudah*. He also wrote explanatory commentaries on the *Shulchan Aruch* and a commentary on several Talmudic tractates.

immediately benefit from this dissection. Rather, the physicians want to learn about this surgery because they might in the future encounter a patient who will require it. Certainly, we cannot override a prohibition for this lesser concern. . . .

For if we were to indeed consider this a case of life and death, it would follow that all forbidden labors on Shabbat would be permitted if they have any medical benefit. [Even if no one were currently ill, it would be permitted to] grind and cook medicines and prepare a knife for bloodletting because of the mere possibility that during Shabbat, or immediately afterward, someone will fall deathly ill and require these things. . . .

If we are permissive about dissection, they will dissect all of our dead simply to study anatomy and know how to treat the living.

QUESTION

Can you detect significant distinctions between the respective decisions of Rabbi Landau and Rabbi Ettlinger?

Watch this in-depth halachic analysis by renowned Jewish legal authority **Rabbi Hershel Schachter** on whether Jewish law recognizes brain death as actual death: **myjli.com/decisions**

TEXT 6A

Handling Scrolls

Talmud, Berachot 18a

וּכְדֶרֶךְ שֶׁאָמְרוּ בַּעֲצָמוֹת, כָּךְ אָמְרוּ בְּסֵפֶר תּוֹרָה.

Just as human bones must be [handled respectfully,] so must a Torah scroll.

TEXT 6B

The Human Torah

Rabbi Yomtov Asevilli, *Chidushei HaRitva*, *Mo'ed Katan* 25a

וְהָרַמְבַּ"ן זַ"ל פֵּרֵשׁ, שֶׁהַנֶּפֶשׁ בַּגּוּף כְּאַזְכָּרוֹת בִּגְוִילִין.

Nachmanides points to the sacred names of G-d that are inked onto a Torah scroll's parchment as an analogy for the sacred soul that is installed within the corporeal body.

RABBI YOMTOV ASEVILLI (RITVA)
C. 1250–1330

Spanish rabbi and Talmudist. Ritva was born in Seville. He is mostly known for his Talmudic commentary, which is extremely clear, and to this day remains most frequently quoted and used.

POGROM
Yissachar Ber Ryback (1837 [Russia]–1935 [Paris]), oil on canvas

TEXT 7

In the Divine Image

Rabbi Dr. J. David Bleich, "Survey of Recent Halakhic Periodical Literature: Cadavers on Display," *Tradition* 40:1 (2007), p. 88

The rationale underlying the regulation mandating respect for the dead . . . is a talmudic parable concerning a pair of twins. One of the twins grows to adulthood and is crowned king of the realm; the second becomes a highwayman, [and] is apprehended and executed as punishment for his crimes. Suppose, then, we are told, the body of the executed twin was placed on public display. Would not passersby scrutinize the body and, perceiving what they believe to be the familiar countenance of their ruler, assume that it is none other than the king himself who has been punished so ignominiously?

Man is created in the image of G-d with the result that, however that anthropomorphic term is to be understood, the human body reflects an aura of divinity. Just as the king is dishonored in the indignity meted out to his twin, G-d is dishonored in the dishonor of the divine image associated with the human body.

RABBI DR. J. DAVID BLEICH 1936–

Expert on Jewish law, ethics, and bioethics. Rabbi Bleich serves as professor of Talmud at the Rabbi Isaac Elchanan Theological Seminary, an affiliate of Yeshiva University, as well as head of its postgraduate institute for the study of Talmudic jurisprudence and family law. A noted author, he is most famous for his 7-volume *Contemporary Halakhic Problems*.

EXERCISE 4.3

When would Rabbi Landau consider autopsy a forbidden desecration of a corpse?

	TO SAVE A LIFE	NOT TO SAVE A LIFE
THE DECEASED CONSENTED		
THE DECEASED DID NOT CONSENT		

TOUCH OF TORAH
Bracha Lavee, felt on canvas, 2005, Israel

TEXT 8

Statistical Danger

Rabbi Dr. J. David Bleich, *Contemporary Halakhic Problems,* vol. IV (New York: Ktav Pub. House/Yeshiva University Press, 1995), pp. 189–191

Although the existence of a presently afflicted patient is an obvious instance in which suspension of halakhic strictures is warranted, it is by no means the only example. . . .

In many outlying settlements in Israel there is but a single qualified health-care provider in residence, usually a nurse. Not infrequently, an emergency occurs on *Shabbat* and, in order to monitor the patient's condition and administer interim medical care, the nurse must accompany the patient in the vehicle transporting the patient to the nearest hospital. During her absence there is no trained professional qualified to provide emergency care should any other inhabitant become afflicted by illness or suffer an accident. May the nurse ignore *Shabbat* prohibitions in order to return to her post? . . .

The likelihood that a child in any specific family will become afflicted with a life-threatening illness on any given *Shabbat* is extremely remote. Hence, the mother's preparations for that eventuality cannot be categorized as an act of *pikuach nefesh*. However, when past experience points to a significant likelihood that one person in a large population of individuals will be stricken in such a manner, a number of rabbinic decisors have ruled that the statistical probability of the occurrence of such an event is sufficient to warrant the nurse's return to her post.

In effect, present awareness of the statistical probability of impending danger renders the danger itself present in nature.

EPIDEMIC IN *SHTETL*
Adam (Aron) Muszka (1914 [Piotrków Trybunalski, Poland]–2005 [Paris])

TEXT 9

Cadaveric Biopsies

Rabbi Moshe Feinstein, *Igrot Moshe, Yoreh De'ah* 2:151

נִרְאֶה לְפִי עֲנִיּוּת דַעְתִּי דְאִם לֹא יַחְתְּכוּ הָאֵבָרִים וְלֹא יִפְתְּחוּ צַוָּארוֹ וּבִטְנוֹ, רַק רוֹצִים לִתְחֹב נִידֶעל לְהוֹצִיא מִמֶּנּוּ אֵיזֶה לַחְלוּחִית לְהִוָּדַע מִזֶּה אֵיזוֹ דְבָרִים הַנּוֹגְעִים לְהַמַּחֲלָה, שֶׁזֶּה אֵין לְהַחֲשִׁיב לְנִוּוּל, שֶׁהֲרֵי דָבָר כָּזֶה מָצוּי טוּבָא בִּזְמַנֵּנוּ שֶׁעוֹשִׂים כֵּן גַּם לַחַיִּים, וְיֵשׁ לְהַתִּיר בִּפְשִׁיטוּת. וְכֵן לְהוֹצִיא מְעַט דָּם לִבְדֹּק וְכַדּוֹמֶה עַל יְדֵי נִידֶעל אֵינוֹ נִוּוּל וְיֵשׁ לְהַתִּיר. וְאַף שֶׁלֹּא מָצָאתִי זֶה בְּפֵרוּשׁ, נִרְאֶה זֶה לְפִי עֲנִיּוּת דַעְתִּי בָּרוּר.

In my opinion, it would not constitute a violation of *nivul* (desecration) if physicians will not cut open the limbs, neck, or torso, but only seek to perform a needle biopsy in order to obtain fluid for diagnostic analysis and evaluation. It is not a form of desecration and is permissible because it is very common to do such procedures on the living. Likewise, removing blood via needle and syringe for analysis does not constitute desecration and is permitted. Although I have not found this stated explicitly in earlier sources, it seems clear to me that this is true.

RABBI MOSHE FEINSTEIN 1895–1986

Leading Halachic authority of the 20th century. Rabbi Feinstein was appointed rabbi of Luban, Belarus, in 1921. He immigrated to the U.S. in 1937 and became the dean of Metivta Tiferet Yerushalayim in New York. Rabbi Feinstein's Halachic decisions have been published in a multivolume collection entitled *Igrot Moshe*.

TEXT 10

Alternative Autopsies

Sudhin Thayyil, et al., "Post-Mortem MRI versus Conventional Autopsy in Fetuses and Children: A Prospective Validation Study," *Lancet*, May 2013

Post-mortem MRI is a potential diagnostic alternative to conventional autopsy, but few large prospective studies have compared its accuracy with that of conventional autopsy. We assessed the accuracy of whole-body, post-mortem MRI for detection of major pathological lesions associated with death in a prospective cohort of fetuses and children. . . .

Minimally invasive autopsy has accuracy similar to that of conventional autopsy for detection of cause of death or major pathological abnormality after death in fetuses, newborns, and infants, but was less accurate in older children. If undertaken jointly by pathologists and radiologists, minimally invasive autopsy could be an acceptable alternative to conventional autopsy in selected cases.

DR. SUDHIN THAYYIL

Neonatologist and researcher. Thayyil conducted the largest prospective study to date on minimally invasive autopsy by postmortem magnetic resonance imaging and was awarded a PhD by University College London for this work.

III. YOU SHALL SURELY BURY

The above discussion of the halachic views on postmortem dissection leads to a second halachic issue raised by the use of cadavers in medical research: the Jewish laws of burial.

TEXT 11

Burial Wishes

Maimonides, *Mishneh Torah*, Laws of Mourning 12:1

אִם צִוָּה שֶׁלֹּא יִקָּבֵר אֵין שׁוֹמְעִין לוֹ, שֶׁהַקְּבוּרָה מִצְוָה, שֶׁנֶּאֱמַר: "כִּי קָבוֹר תִּקְבְּרֶנּוּ" (דְבָרִים כא, כג).

If the deceased had instructed that they not be buried after their death, we do not obey, because we are commanded to bury our dead, as the verse states, "You shall bury them on that same day" (DEUTERONOMY 21:23).

RABBI MOSHE BEN MAIMON (MAIMONIDES, RAMBAM) 1135–1204

Halachist, philosopher, author, and physician. Maimonides was born in Córdoba, Spain. After the conquest of Córdoba by the Almohads, he fled Spain and eventually settled in Cairo, Egypt. There, he became the leader of the Jewish community and served as court physician to the vizier of Egypt. He is most noted for authoring the *Mishneh Torah*, an encyclopedic arrangement of Jewish law; and for his philosophical work, *Guide for the Perplexed*. His rulings on Jewish law are integral to the formation of Halachic consensus.

TEXT 12

Returning the Deposit

Rabbi Chaim Vital, *Etz Hadaat Tov* 358 (Jerusalem, 2008 edition)

"כִּי עָפָר אַתָּה וְאֶל עָפָר תָּשׁוּב" (בְּרֵאשִׁית ג, יט). כִּי גוּף הָאָדָם מִן הֶעָפָר הָיָה, וְדֶרֶךְ פִּקָּדוֹן הָפְקַד בְּיַד הָאָדָם. וּכְשֶׁמֵּת צָרִיךְ לְהַחֲזִיר הַפִּקָּדוֹן אֶל הֶעָפָר אֲשֶׁר מִמֶּנּוּ לֻקַּח וּלְקוֹבְרוֹ.

"For you were made from dust, and to dust you will return" (GENESIS 3:19). The human body was created from the earth and our bodies are handed to us as a deposit. Upon death, the deposit must be returned to the earth, from where it was taken, for burial.

RABBI CHAIM VITAL
C. 1542–1620

Lurianic kabbalist. Rabbi Vital was born in Israel, lived in Safed and Jerusalem, and later lived in Damascus. He was authorized by his teacher, Rabbi Yitzchak Luria, the Arizal, to record his teachings. Acting on this mandate, Vital began arranging his master's teachings in written form, and his many works constitute the foundation of the Lurianic school of Jewish mysticism. His most famous work is *Etz Chayim*.

Memorial reminder, artist unknown, paint on cut-out paper, with typewritten inscriptions. Gardiner, Maine, c. 1915. The writing on this artwork mentions "Shime, daughter of Solomon David," whose passing was in late 1915. (The Jewish Museum, New York, N.Y.)

TEXT 13

Full Burial

Rabbi Yehudah Meir Shapiro, *Or Hameir* 74:5

דַאֲפִלוּ לְמִי שֶׁצִּדֵּד לְהַתִּיר בִּשְׁאֵלָה דְנִוּוּל הַמֵּת, בְּנִדּוֹן דִּידַן אֵין צַד הֶתֵּר כְּלָל. כִּי חָקַרְנוּ וְדָרַשְׁנוּ הֵיטֵב, וְהִנֵּה נוֹדַע לָנוּ כִּי בִּמְלֶאכֶת הַפְּרָאזֶעקְטוֹרְיוּם, אֵבָרִים רַבִּים שֶׁל מֵת אֵינָם בָּאִים כְּלָל לִקְבוּרָה, מֵהֶם נִשְׁלָקִים, וּמֵהֶם נִגְנָזִים בְּכֵלִים, וְהֵם מְסֻמָּנִים בְּמִסְפָּרִים . . .

וְהַדָּבָר מְבֹאָר בִּירוּשַׁלְמִי נָזִיר (ז, א): "תִּקְבְּרֶנּוּ" כֻּלּוֹ וְלֹא מִקְצָתוֹ. "תִּקְבְּרֶנוּ" מִכַּן שֶׁאִם שִׁיֵּר מִמֶּנּוּ לֹא עָשָׂה כְּלוּם.

Even those opinions that tend to be more lenient regarding the question of desecrating the dead would agree that there is no permission [to provide bodies to the medical schools in Poland]. We have done an investigation into the protocols of the prosectorium and have learned that many of the limbs of bodies donated to these medical schools are never buried. Some are scalded, some are stored in containers, and some are branded with numerals. . . .

The Jerusalem Talmud (NAZIR 7:1) states: "When the Torah commands, 'Bury them,' it is instructing us to bury the entire corpse. This informs us that if part of the body is left unburied, it is as if no burial has occurred."

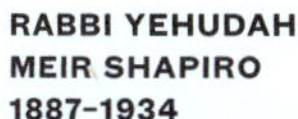

RABBI YEHUDAH MEIR SHAPIRO 1887–1934

Leader of Polish Jewry during the interwar years. Rabbi Shapiro was born in Shatz, Romania. He accepted his first rabbinic post at age 23 in Galina, Poland. In 1923, he initiated the idea of *daf yomi,* or "daily folio," the regimen of learning one folio of the Babylonian Talmud each day, completing the 2,711 pages every 7½ years. He founded the famous Chachmei Lublin yeshiva in 1924.

Why does Judaism put such great importance on burying our dead? **Rabbi Raleigh Resnick** explains: **myjli.com/decisions**

The requirement to bury the body in its entirety raises the question of cadaveric transplants. For details about this, see Appendix.

TEXT 14

Body and Soul Rest

Midrash, *Vayikra Rabah* 18:1

"וְיָשֹׁב הֶעָפָר עַל הָאָרֶץ כְּשֶׁהָיָה וְגוֹ'" (קֹהֶלֶת יב, ז) . . .

אֵימָתַי הָרוּחַ תָּשׁוּב אֶל הָאֱלֹקִים אֲשֶׁר נְתָנָהּ?
כְּשֶׁשָּׁב הֶעָפָר אֶל הָאָרֶץ כְּשֶׁהָיָה.

"The dust returns to the earth as it was [at the start of Creation], and the spirit returns to G-d Who gave it" (ECCLESIASTES 12:7). . . .

When does the spirit return to G-d Who gave it? When the dust returns to the earth as it was.

VAYIKRA RABAH

An early rabbinic commentary on the Book of Leviticus. This Midrash, written in Aramaic and Hebrew, provides textual exegeses and anecdotes, expounds upon the biblical narrative, and develops and illustrates moral principles. It was first printed in Constantinople in 1512 together with 4 other Midrashic works on the other 4 books of the Pentateuch.

DIGGING THE GRAVE
Artist unknown: from a cycle of paintings created for the *Chevrah Kadisha* (Jewish Burial Society) of Prague, oil on canvas, c. 1772, Prague

IV. CONCLUSION

All of the above enables us to summarize the position of Jewish law regarding autopsies and postmortem dissection in the process of medical training and research.

TEXT 15

Religious Accommodation

New York Consolidated Laws, Public Health Law - PBH § 4210-c: Limitations to Dissection or Autopsy

In the absence of a compelling public necessity, no dissection or autopsy shall be performed over the objection of a surviving relative or friend of the deceased that such procedure is contrary to the religious belief of the decedent, or, if there is otherwise reason to believe that a dissection or autopsy is contrary to the decedent's religious beliefs. . . .

"Compelling public necessity" shall mean: (i) that the dissection or autopsy is essential to the conduct of a criminal investigation of a homicide . . . of which the decedent is the victim, or (ii) that discovery of the cause of death is necessary to meet an immediate and substantial threat to the public health and that a dissection or autopsy is essential to ascertain the cause of death. . . .

All dissections or autopsies performed pursuant to this section shall be the least intrusive procedure consistent with the compelling state interest.

QUESTION

Based on the Jewish sources presented earlier, might it be permissible according to Jewish law to use unclaimed bodies for anatomical dissection?

Pages from the year 5694 (1934) from a handwritten record book of the Miskolc, Hungary, Jewish Burial Society from 1934–1942. The National Library of Israel and the Hungarian Jewish Museum and Archives saved this book from being auctioned in 2021.

TEXT 16

Burying the Unclaimed

Maimonides, *Mishneh Torah,* Laws of Mourning 3:8

כֹּהֵן שֶׁפָּגַע בְּמֵת מִצְוָה בַּדֶּרֶךְ, הֲרֵי זֶה מִטַּמֵּא לוֹ.
אֲפִלּוּ כֹּהֵן גָּדוֹל חַיָּב לְהִטַּמֵּא לוֹ וּלְקוֹבְרוֹ.

וְאֵיזֶהוּ מֵת מִצְוָה? אֶחָד מִיִּשְׂרָאֵל שֶׁהָיָה
מֻשְׁלָךְ בַּדֶּרֶךְ וְאֵין לוֹ קוֹבְרִין.

When a *Kohen* (a member of the Jewish priestly family)—even the *Kohen Gadol* (highest priest)—encounters a *met mitzvah* on the road, he is obligated to become ritually impure for the sake of burying it.

What constitutes a *met mitzvah*? A Jewish corpse cast along the road with no one to bury it.

JEWISH FUNERAL IN VILNIUS [LITHUANIA] IN 1824
Julian Karczewski, oil on canvas, 1824 (National Museum in Warsaw)

KEY POINTS

1 Human beings have an interest in the integrity of their bodies in death as in life. An unwarranted desecration of the dead is akin to theft.

2 The human body reflects an aura of Divinity in death as in life. We are granted certain rights over our bodies, but we have no right to consent to bodily denigration because G-d is thereby dishonored.

3 When G-d reclaims the breath of life, we ought to return the body—a deposit granted to humans—to the ground, the place from which G-d fashioned the first human being, without delay. The soul does not reach its final rest until the body is buried.

4 Normally, the obligation to bury the dead lies with the family of the deceased. But when a body is found abandoned, we all have an obligation to care for it and bring it to proper burial.

5 It is becoming more common for pathologists to perform "virtual autopsies." This alternative, along with other noninvasive postmortem procedures, is far preferable to the traditional invasive autopsy, which Jewish law, subject to certain limited exceptions, generally prohibits.

6 When performing a permitted postmortem procedure, care should be taken to do so in the most dignified and respectful way possible.

Grave Robbery and the Jewish Response

The following collection of texts explores the tumultuous history of anatomical dissection and its impact on the Jewish community. As the practice gained prominence during the Renaissance, the demand for human cadavers skyrocketed, leading to a dark era of body snatching and grave robbery. Throughout Europe and America, Jewish communities were also targeted, forcing them to take drastic measures to protect their cemeteries. Here we examine the rise of grave robbery, one community's extraordinary response, and the legal solution that ended America's illicit trade in disinterred bodies.

SCHACHNUS CEMETERY
(SCHACHNUS BET TEFILAH CEMETERY)
Orthodox Jewish cemetery established in 1874 by Congregation Bet Tefilah, then led by Rabbi Schachne Isaacs, for whom the cemetery is named, Cincinnati, Ohio

The Rise of Grave Robbery

Rabbi Edward Reichman, M.D., "The Anatomy of Halakha," in Y. Steinberg, ed., *Beracha Le'Avraham* (Jerusalem: 2008), pp. 69–97

With the incorporation of systematic anatomical dissection into medical training in the Renaissance, a need for the supply of human cadavers rapidly developed. As there was initially no legal means of obtaining such specimens, the universities employed novel procurement methods. In certain cases, medical students were obliged to provide cadavers from their respective communities. This demand impacted the Jewish medical students and the broader Jewish community, who obviously opposed the desecration of the body for this purpose.

The demand for Jewish bodies continued into the twentieth century throughout Europe. In Warsaw in the 1920s, the medical school requested Jewish bodies for dissection—which some community members were willing to provide, lest refusal lead to exclusion of Jewish students from medical training or, worse, to larger anti-Jewish backlash. Rabbi Chaim Elazar Spira (1871–1937), the Munkatch Rebbe, vehemently opposed this acquiescence. Likewise, at Denver's Tuberculosis Hospital in 1916, rabbis refused to furnish Jewish bodies for dissection.

Grave robbing was by no means restricted to Europe. American Jewish communities faced similar issues. Following the Civil War, for instance, an unprecedented enrollment in Ohio medical schools led to great demand for cadavers. With no other recourse, schools turned to professional body snatchers, or "resurrectionists." Roughly five thousand bodies were exhumed in Ohio in the nineteenth century for dissection purposes. Unique patents for devices designed to prevent grave robbing were submitted from this state. These included a terra cotta burial case and the "torpedo" coffin, the latter rigged with explosives set to detonate upon disturbance of the casket.

Rabbi Schachne Isaacs (1815–1887) emigrated to the U.S. from Lithuania around 1856 and founded the Bet Tefilah Synagogue in Cincinnati, Ohio, in 1866.

The Grisly Dilemma

Letter of Rabbi Schachne Isaacs to Rabbi Bentzion Sternfeld, *Shaarei Tziyon* 1:31

In our city [Cincinnati], there is a terrible plague, the mere mention of which causes one's ears to ring. There are several local medical schools with students studying anatomy, for which they require human cadavers. It has come to light that they have removed hundreds, even thousands of bodies from their graves. Moreover, they have commercialized this, as they preserve the bodies and send them to other states.

[To protect against such robberies,] the non-Jews have made caves adjacent to their cemeteries, wherein they carve out cavities to place the bodies temporarily until reinterment in the summer.

The wealthy among the Jewish community arrange for watchmen over their graves, but only for a few days because our cemetery is about four miles from where we live, which makes hiring a guard very expensive. Even this is for naught, as we have spoken with physicians who state that even two to three weeks after burial, the bodies are still useful for dissection and that doctors are willing to spend large sums of money to get such bodies.

We, therefore, ask if we may do as [our non-Jewish neighbors and build temporary burial structures]. This is a novel matter, and we do not wish to act on our own authority. . . . We would like to build a structure in the cemetery with a stone floor and an iron door. In it, we would construct compartments in which to deposit bodies temporarily until permanent burial can take place in the summer.

Rabbi Benzion Sternfeld (1835–1914) served as rabbi of the communities of Chislavichi, Bielsk, and Kalvarija in Eastern Europe from the late 1860s until his passing. He authored a three-volume work, *Shaarei Tziyon*, consisting of essays on Talmudic logic and halachic responsa.

Rabbinic Response

Response of Rabbi Bentzion Sternfeld, *Shaarei Tziyon* 1:31

You proposed the construction of temporary burial compartments below the ground, into which the coffin will be placed. If so, this is considered proper burial . . . and it is acceptable in my opinion. This is on condition that the compartments are actually dug into the ground. If you need to build walls to prevent the compartments from collapsing, you may do so, but the floor of the compartment must be the actual earth. If the floor is not earth then this would be like interring the body in a house, and would not be considered burial.

The Fall of Grave Robbery

Ann Garment, et al., "Let the Dead Teach the Living: The Rise of Body Bequeathal in 20th-Century America," *Academic Medicine* 82:10 (October 2007), p. 1001

The impossibility of obtaining enough cadavers legally made legislative revision inevitable. Massachusetts became the first state to enact a solution—using unclaimed bodies for dissection—and, in 1830 and 1833, passed laws permitting dissection of the unclaimed dead. Over the ensuing decades, many other states passed their own anatomy acts following the example of Massachusetts, providing that the unclaimed bodies of people who died in public institutions—hospitals, asylums, and prisons—would go to the state's medical schools.

Because burying unclaimed bodies had previously used the states' resources, the states, as well as the medical schools, seemed to benefit when those bodies were used for dissection. Few influential voices complained about what happened to unclaimed bodies, and a vocal minority made the point that dissection offered criminals and paupers the opportunity to compensate society for the burden they had caused during their lifetimes. As one *Washington Post* editorialist asked in 1887, "Why would those who have made war on society or have been a burden to it be permitted to say what shall be done with their remains? Why should they not be compelled to be of some use after death, having failed to be of value to the world during life?"

BODY SNATCHERS AT WORK
Artist unknown: painting on wood, at the Old Crown Inn (located close to the town graveyard), Penicuik, Midlothian, Scotland

The Value of Honoring the Deceased

Jewish law considers the human body a sacred entity and mandates that it be treated with honor and dignity. The following collection of texts describes the body's sanctity and the manner in which it should be honored.

Sanctity

TALMUD, MO'ED KATAN 25A

If you are present at the time of a person's passing, you must rend your clothing. This is because a person's demise is likened to the burning of a Torah scroll [and observers of the Torah's desecration must rend their clothing in mourning].

RABBI YOMTOV ASEVILLI (RITVA), MO'ED KATAN 25A

Nachmanides explained that the soul installed within the body is like the Divine names inscribed on the parchment of a Torah scroll.

RABBI MOSHE SOFER,
CHATAM SOFER, YOREH DE'AH 353

Humans are created in G-d's image. . . . Just as we draw no distinction between desecration of an entire Torah scroll and desecration of a single letter in a Torah scroll, so are we prohibited from displaying disrespect to even a single bone from a sacred body that was created in G-d's image.

RABBI YOSEF SHAUL NATANSON,
YAD SHAUL, YOREH DE'AH 340:5

The Talmud (Avodah Zarah 18a) relates that when the Romans wrapped Rabbi Chananyah ben Tradyon in a Torah scroll and burned him alive, his students asked him, "What do you see?" He replied, "The parchment burns, but the letters fly up to the Heavens!"

Only the physical parchment burned, but the letters—being spiritual entities—flew up to Heaven. . . . Similarly, each person is comprised of matter and spirit. When a person's life ends, only their corporeal body dies, whereas their soul ascends to its original home.

Honor

RABBI YECHIEL MICHEL TUKACHINSKY, *GESHER HACHAYIM* 5:4

We maintain watch over the freshly deceased until burial . . . out of respect. If we were to leave the body alone, it would appear as if we had abandoned it like some utensil whose usefulness has expired and is therefore no longer desired.

TALMUD, BERACHOT 18A

Rachava taught in the name of Rav Yehudah: One who witnesses a corpse being taken for burial and does not accompany the funeral procession transgresses the prohibition, "Those who mock the poor insult their Creator" (Proverbs 17:5). Conversely, if we escort the deceased, what is our reward? Rav Asi said: Of such a person, the verse declares, "Those who pity the poor lend to G-d, and G-d will repay them" (Proverbs 19:17), and "Those who are kind to the poor honor G-d" (Proverbs 14:31).

RABBI YECHIEL MICHEL TUKACHINSKY, *GESHER HACHAYIM* 5:1

All who handle the deceased must be aware that they are dealing with a sacred entity. A human body is not only a "container" that held an exalted soul; rather, the body became sanctified with a sanctity of its own, similar to the sanctity that belongs to the parchment of a Torah scroll.

TALMUD, KETUBOT 17A

Our sages taught, "We must suspend our Torah study to attend the burial of a corpse and a wedding." Indeed, the sages reported that the great Rabbi Yehudah son of Rabbi Elai would suspend his Torah study to attend the burial of a corpse and a wedding.

When does the above hold true? When there are not enough people attending a corpse to properly provide the honor due to the deceased. However, if there are enough people attending to meet all of the requirements, we are not obligated to suspend our Torah study.

TALMUD, MEGILAH 29A

Our Sages taught: We may not act flippantly in a cemetery, we may not graze an animal there, we may not direct a water channel through it, and we may not gather hay for animals there. If someone gathered hay inside a cemetery, it should be burned on the spot. This is in order to show respect for the dead.

MAIMONIDES, *MISHNEH TORAH*, LAWS OF MOURNING 3:8

When a priest—even the High Priest—encounters a *met mitzvah* on the road [between inhabited areas], he must defile himself for its sake and bury it.

What is a *met mitzvah*? A Jewish corpse lying haplessly on the roadside with no one around to bury it.

APPENDIX

TEXT 17

Benefiting from the Dead

Maimonides, *Mishneh Torah*, Laws of Mourning 14:21

הַמֵּת אָסוּר בַּהֲנָאָה כֻּלּוֹ, חוּץ מִשְּׂעָרוֹ שֶׁהוּא מֻתָּר בַּהֲנָאָה מִפְּנֵי שֶׁאֵינוֹ גּוּפוֹ. וְכֵן אֲרוֹנוֹ וְכָל תַּכְרִיכָיו אֲסוּרִין בַּהֲנָאָה.

It is forbidden to derive benefit from any part of the dead. One may, however, derive benefit from the hair because it is not considered part of the body. It is also forbidden to derive benefit from the coffin or any of the shrouds.

MAKING THE SHROUD
Artist unknown: from a cycle of paintings created for the *Chevrah Kadisha* (Jewish Burial Society) of Prague, oil on canvas, c. 1772, Prague

TEXT 18

Resurrected Organs

Rabbi Isser Yehudah Unterman, *Shevet MiYehudah,* pp. 55–56

בְּשַׂר הַמֵּת אָסוּר רַק כָּל זְמַן שֶׁהוּא מֵת. וּכְשֶׁהֵקִיץ לִתְחִיָּה, נִפְקַע הָאִסּוּר מִמֵּילָא.

וּכְמוֹ שֶׁאֵין מָקוֹם לַחֲשֹׁב כִּי בְּהַמְאֹרָעוֹת שֶׁל תְּחִיַּת הַמֵּתִים הַנִּזְכָּרִים בַּתָּנָ"ךְ . . . הָיוּ הָאֲנָשִׁים הַלָּלוּ אֲסוּרִים בַּהֲנָאָה, כֵּן גַּם בְּחֵלֶק מִן הַמֵּת שֶׁשָּׁב וַיְחִי עַל יְדֵי חִבּוּר עִם גּוּף חַי, אֵין אִסּוּר הֲנָאָה. וְהַטַּעַם הוּא מִפְּנֵי שֶׁסִּבַּת הָאִסּוּר שֶׁל בְּשַׂר הַמֵּת הִיא לֹא בְּמָה שֶׁיָּצְאָה נִשְׁמָתוֹ קֹדֶם, אֶלָּא בְּזֶה שֶׁהוּא עַכְשָׁו מֵת . . .

וְהַסְבָּרָא מִתְקַבֶּלֶת עַל הַדַּעַת כְּשֶׁנִּקַּח לָנוּ לְדֻגְמָא אֶת דִּין הַטֻּמְאָה שֶׁל בְּשַׂר הַמֵּת. כִּי נִרְאֶה לִי פָּשׁוּט, שֶׁאִם אֶחָד עָשָׂה נִתּוּחַ כָּזֶה מִגּוּף מֵת שֶׁל יְהוּדִי שֶׁחִבֵּר לְגוּפוֹ, אֵינוֹ מְטַמֵּא בְּאֹהֶל, וּמֻתָּר לְכֹהֵן לִכָּנֵס לְבַיִת זֶה שֶׁהָאִישׁ נִמְצָא בְּתוֹכוֹ . . . וְאִם בְּדִין טֻמְאָה כֵּן, מִסְתַּבֵּר לוֹמַר שֶׁגַּם בְּנוֹגֵעַ לְאִסּוּר הֲנָאָה הַדִּין כֵּן . . .

כְּמוֹ כֵן, הֵעִיר רַב חָשׁוּב שֶׁאִי אֶפְשָׁר לְהִשְׁתַּמֵּשׁ בִּבְשַׂר הַמֵּת לִרְפוּאָה מִפְּנֵי שֶׁיֵּשׁ מִצְוָה לְקָבְרוֹ. אֲבָל אֵין מְנִיעָה מִצַּד זֶה, שֶׁהֲרֵי כְּשֶׁמַּחֲזִירִים לוֹ אֶת חִיּוּתוֹ עַל יְדֵי חִבּוּר לְגוּף אַחֵר, אֵין חִיּוּב קְבוּרָה עַל זֶה. וּכְמוֹ שֶׁאֵין לִשְׁאֹל עַל תְּחִיַּת בֶּן הַשּׁוּנַמִּית הֲלֹא חַיָּב הוּא לְהִקָּבֵר, כֵּן אֵין זֶה מְעַכֵּב עַל תְּחִיַּת חֵלֶק מִמֶּנּוּ.

RABBI ISSER YEHUDAH UNTERMAN 1886–1976

Second Ashkenazi chief rabbi of the State of Israel. Rabbi Unterman was born in Brest-Litovsk, Belarus. In 1923, he assumed the rabbinate of Liverpool, England. During World War II, he worked to relieve the plight of the Jewish refugees who had escaped from Nazi Germany and settled in England. In 1946, Rabbi Unterman became chief rabbi of Tel Aviv-Jaffa. In 1964, he was appointed as the Ashkenazi chief rabbi of the State of Israel.

Watch *Brain Death and Organ Transplants,* an informative lecture by **Rabbi Yitzchak Breitowitz**: **myjli.com/decisions**

The flesh from the dead is forbidden only as long as it remains lifeless. When it comes back to life, the prohibition is automatically lifted.

It is unthinkable to argue that it would have been forbidden to derive benefit . . . from the biblical figures who were resurrected. So too, when a dead body part returns to life by being transplanted into a living body, there is no prohibition against benefiting from it. This is because the ban against benefiting from the dead applies not to flesh that once experienced death, but rather to that which is currently dead. . . .

Burial prayer pages from a miscellany [collection of prayers] for life cycle events; ink on parchment, Leon ben Joshua de Rossi of Cesena, copyist, last third of the 15th century, Italy (possibly Ferrara) (Braginsky Collection)

This logic appears quite reasonable in light of the laws of the ritual impurity imparted by a corpse. It is obvious that a person who receives a transplant from a cadaver does not render others in their presence ritually impure. A *Kohen* would be permitted to enter the same room as the transplant recipient. . . . If this is so regarding the laws of ritual impurity, it seems likely that the same would apply to the prohibition of deriving benefit from the dead. . . .

A prominent rabbi noted that, because of the obligation to bury the deceased, the flesh of the dead cannot be used for medical purposes. But this obligation does not pose a problem for transplants because when an organ returns to life when it is implanted in another body, it no longer needs to be buried. Just as the son of the Shunamite did not need to be buried after he was revived, a transplanted organ does not require burial.

Jewish medical ethicist **Rabbi Edward Reichman, M.D.** discusses organ donation: **myjli.com/decisions**

Select U.S. Law

Lesson One

SELECT U.S. LAW RELATED TO THE RIGHT TO TRY

The *Trickett Wendler, Frank Mongiello, Jordan McLinn and Matthew Bellina Right to Try Act of 2017*, also known as the U.S. Right to Try Act, created a uniform system for terminal patients seeking access to investigational treatments.

This act provides a path for patients who have been diagnosed with life-threatening diseases or conditions—who have tried all approved treatment options and who are unable to participate in a clinical trial—to access certain investigational treatment options.

It allows experimental drugs to be administered to terminally ill patients who have exhausted all approved treatment options and are unable to participate in clinical drug trials. All eligible drugs must have undergone the Food and Drug Administration's (FDA) Phase I (safety) testing. The law seeks to increase access to experimental medications by allowing patients, through their physicians, to request experimental medicines directly from drug manufacturers without involving the FDA. The FDA's expanded access program exists in parallel with the Right to Try Act.

Currently, 41 states have enacted Right to Try laws, several of them enacted during the years before the Federal version.

BACKGROUND

In the United States, all drugs must be approved by the United States **Food and Drug Administration** (FDA or U.S. FDA), a federal agency within the Department of Health and Human Services (HHS) having the authority to oversee the quality of substances sold as drugs or as food in the United States and to monitor claims made in labeling both the composition and the health benefits of foods.

An extensive, rigorous process is required to get a new drug approved by the FDA. However, the FDA may skip the extensive FDA process usually required, in order to expeditiously approve drugs under certain exceptional circumstances. These exceptions utilize the public policy concepts known as Expanded Access and Emergency Use Authorization.

The FDA's official term, Expanded Access (often commonly referred to as Compassionate Use),[1] refers to permitting a seriously ill patient, under certain conditions, to try a new, unapproved (and otherwise illegal) drug when no other treatments are available. Drugs being tested but not approved by the FDA are called investigational drugs. These drugs are ordinarily available only to people participating in a clinical trial.

Another type of exception to the FDA approval process occurs when the Secretary of HHS declares that an Emergency Use Authorization is appropriate. The FDA may then authorize unapproved medical products or unapproved uses of approved medical products to be used in an emergency to diagnose, treat, or prevent serious or life-threatening diseases or conditions caused by chemical, biological, radiological, and nuclear (CBRN) threats when certain criteria are met, including when there are no adequate, approved, and available alternatives. (See 21 U.S. Code § 360bbb-3: Authorization for medical products for use in emergencies.)

For example, in early 2020, then-HHS Secretary Alex Azar declared that during the COVID-19 pandemic, circumstances existed justifying the authorization of emergency use of certain drugs and biological products. After this declaration, the FDA authorized the use of several COVID-19 vaccines, pursuant to Secretary Azar's abovementioned Emergency Use Authorization.

IMPORTANT CASES

Pioneering cases preceding the 2018 passage and signing-into-law of the Federal Right to Try Act of 2017 concerned using experimental or unconventional therapies in treating serious illnesses *or* illegally obtaining and using marijuana or other then-illegal

1. Terminology for describing pre-approval mechanisms or programs may vary by country or even by drug manufacturer. They include: Managed Access Program (MAP), Expanded Access Program (EAP), Named Patient Supply (NPS), Compassionate Use Program (CUP) and many others. In the U.S., the terms Expanded Access and Compassionate Use are used interchangeably. However, for a thorough understanding of the distinctions between the terms Expanded Access, Compassionate Use, Right to Try, and other relevant terms, see "Understanding Expanded Access, Compassionate Use and Similar Terms," *myTomorrows*, May 18, 2020, at link.myjli.com/dof4_k.

substances to treat their conventional therapies' debilitating side effects. These patients' actions sometimes led to their arrest by state or local law authorities. In such cases, individuals suffering from these illnesses (or from conventional medicine's side effects) have argued in court that they *were* legally permitted to use such drugs, even though the relevant agencies had not approved them. Here are two such cases and the courts' decisions.

Abigail Alliance for Better Access to Developmental Drugs v. von Eschenbach, 495 F.3d 695 (D.C. Cir. 2007), cert denied, 552 U.S. 1159 (2008)

In this case, the plaintiff argued grounds of self-defense, necessity, and interference with rescue, in seeking to use an experimental drug. The Circuit Court for the District of Columbia considered whether patients have a right to use "a potentially toxic drug with no proven therapeutic benefit," deciding against the plaintiff. The drug in question was an experimental drug being tested to treat colon cancer, which the plaintiff sought to use to treat terminal head-and-neck cancer.

The Supreme Court declined to hear an appeal of the Circuit Court's ruling, which had reversed a U.S. Court of Appeals for the District of Columbia's ruling in favor of the plaintiff. Thus, the Circuit Court's decision remained in place, denying the use of the drug.

United States v. Randall, 171 F.3d 195 (4th Cir. 1999)[2]

This case led to the delineation of criteria for defendants to invoke an important concept in Right to Try: the necessity defense. The defendant suffered from a painful illness that experts had determined could be treated with medical drugs or surgery. Experts

---

2. Other landmark cases concerning palliative and other medical uses of marijuana include:

   United States v. Oakland Cannabis Buyers' Cooperative, 532 U.S. 483 (2001). In this case the Supreme Court ruled that there is no *medical necessity* exception to the Controlled Substances Act of 1970 prohibitions on manufacturing and distributing marijuana.

   Gonzales v. Raich (previously *Ashcroft v. Raich*), 545 U.S. 1 (2005). The U.S. Supreme Court held that under the Commerce Clause of the U.S. Constitution (Article 1, Section 8, Clause 3), Congress may criminalize the production and use of homegrown cannabis even if state law allows its use for medicinal purposes.

had suggested that the inhalation of marijuana would reduce the pain of his condition. According to the experts' determination, the defendant began smoking marijuana, which was illegal at the time.

The defendant was arrested for possession of marijuana, but he asserted necessity as a defense to his prosecution. In some situations, the necessity defense allows a defendant to engage in illegal activity to prevent serious harm. In such a situation, the defense of necessity, also called the "lesser of two evils" defense, may come into play. A defendant using the necessity defense would usually be obligated to pay for his action if it harmed another but would not be liable for punitive damages or jail time.

The Court held that a defendant may assert the defense of necessity by proving: (1) the defendant believes there is an specific and imminent actual threat and did not themselves bring about the duress or circumstances, (2) the same objective cannot be realistically accomplished in an alternative manner, and (3) the evil (illness or other condition) sought to be averted is more heinous than the criminal act performed to avert that evil.

Lesson Two

SELECT U.S. LAW RELATED TO THE RIGHT TO DIE

Does a person have the right to refuse treatment? Should suicide be legal? Should DNRs (Do Not Resuscitate orders) be respected? Should a doctor be guilty of a crime if they assist a willing patient to commit suicide or they euthanize a patient?

What does the U.S. Constitution say? We will examine several relevant cases in which Due Process is at issue.[3]

The clause in the Fifth Amendment to the United States Constitution provides: "No person shall . . . be deprived of life, liberty, or property, without due process of law" (U.S. Const., amend. V). The clause in Section One of the Fourteenth Amendment to the United States Constitution provides: ". . . nor shall any State deprive any person of life, liberty, or property, without due process of law" (U.S. Const., amend. XIV, § 1).

EUTHANASIA AND ASSISTED SUICIDE

Euthanasia is the term describing when a doctor (or someone else) causes the painless death of a patient—with the patient's prior consent, said consent often given long before the patient is incapacitated—to relieve suffering from an incurable and painful disease or when the person is in an irreversible coma. This practice is currently illegal in all fifty of the United States.

In contrast, *assisted suicide* is the term for when someone, usually a physician, helps a patient to end their own life.

For example, if a doctor administered a lethal drug to a patient, that would be considered euthanasia. However, if the doctor provides the drug to the patient who ingests it on their own, it would be considered assisted suicide. Since 1994, numerous states in the U.S. have passed assisted suicide laws. The law in these states permits terminally ill

3. Due Process Clauses are found in both the Fifth and Fourteenth Amendments to the United States Constitution, which each prohibit the deprivation of "life, liberty, or property" by the federal and state governments, respectively, without due process of law.

adult patients to seek lethal medication from their physicians. Assisted suicide is legal in eleven jurisdictions in the U.S.

The Supreme Court has addressed these issues in a wide range of cases throughout the years.

***Cruzan v. Director, Missouri Department of Health*, 497 U.S. 261 (1990)**

The U.S. Supreme Court found that under the Due Process Clause of the Fifth and Fourteenth Amendments,[4] a person has a constitutional right to refuse all lifesaving medical treatments, irrespective of the patient's prognosis.

The Court found in favor of the Missouri Department of Health. It ruled that nothing in the Constitution prevents the state of Missouri from requiring "clear and convincing evidence" before terminating life-supporting treatment, upholding the ruling of the Missouri Supreme Court.

The Court ruled that, under the Due Process Clause, competent individuals have the right to refuse medical treatment. However, with incompetent individuals, the Court upheld the state of Missouri's higher standard for evidence of what the person would want if they were able to make their own decisions. The Court ruled that this higher evidentiary standard was constitutional because family members might not always make decisions that the incompetent person would have agreed with. Those decisions might lead to actions (like withdrawing life support) that would be irreversible.

***Compassion in Dying v. Washington, 79 F. 3d 790, 798 (1996); Washington v. Glucksberg*, 521 U.S. 702 (1997); *Vacco v. Quill*, 521 U.S. 793 (1997)**

In *Compassion in Dying v. Washington*, the U.S. Court of Appeals for the Ninth Circuit held that physician-assisted suicide is a fundamental right under the Due Process Clause of the Fourteenth Amendment.

---

4. The Due Process Clause prohibits the deprivation of "life, liberty, or property" by the federal and state governments, respectively, without due process of law. The U.S. Supreme Court interprets these clauses to guarantee a variety of protections.

However, in *Washington v. Glucksberg* and *Vacco v. Quill,* the U.S. Supreme Court reversed the Appellate Courts, holding that there is no right to physician-assisted suicide under the Equal Protection or Due Process clauses of the Fifth and Fourteenth Amendments.

Lesson Three

SELECT U.S. LAW RELATED TO ABORTION

Over the years, there has been much litigation regarding the legality of abortion in the United States. Landmark abortion rulings include *Roe v. Wade,* in 1973; *Planned Parenthood of Southeastern Pa. v. Casey,* in 1992; and the more recent *Dobbs v. Jackson Women's Health Organization,* in 2022, which overturned both *Roe* and *Casey.*

Roe v. Wade, 410 U.S. 113, 132-34 (1973)

In *Roe v. Wade,* the U.S. Supreme Court ruled that the Constitution of the United States generally protects a pregnant woman's liberty to have an abortion. The decision struck down many states' abortion laws and sparked an ongoing abortion debate in the United States about whether or to what extent abortion should be legal, who should decide the legality of abortion, and the role of moral and religious views in the political sphere.

The plaintiff, Norma McCorvey (under the legal pseudonym Jane Roe), was a resident of Texas, where abortion was illegal except when necessary to save the mother's life. Roe argued that Texas abortion laws were unconstitutional.

In a 7–2 decision, the Supreme Court held that the Due Process Clause of the Fourteenth Amendment to the United States Constitution provides a fundamental "right to privacy,"[5] which protects a pregnant woman's right to an abortion. It also held that the right to abortion is not absolute and must be balanced against the government's interests in protecting women's health and prenatal life. It resolved these competing interests by announcing a pregnancy-trimester timetable to govern all abortion regulations in the United States. During the first trimester, the decision to terminate the pregnancy was solely at the woman's discretion. After the first trimester, the state could

---

5. The 14th Amendment of the U.S. Constitution states, "No state shall make or enforce any law which shall abridge the privileges or immunities of citizens of the United States; nor shall any state deprive any person of life, liberty, or property, without due process of law; nor deny to any person within its jurisdiction the equal protection of the laws" (U.S. Const. amend. XIV, § 1).

"regulate procedure." During the second trimester, the state could regulate (but not outlaw) abortions in the interests of the mother's health.

***Planned Parenthood of Southeastern Pa. v. Casey*, 505 U.S. 833 (1992)**

In *Planned Parenthood of Southeastern Pa. v. Casey*, the Supreme Court upheld the right to have an abortion as established by the "essential holding" of *Roe v. Wade* (1973) and issued, as its "key judgment," the imposition of the undue burden standard when evaluating state-imposed restrictions on that right.

While retaining the "essential holding" in *Roe* and acknowledging that women had some constitutional liberty to terminate their pregnancies, the Court overturned the *Roe* trimester framework. Rather, they favored an analysis of fetal viability.

The *Roe* trimester framework had regulations designed to protect a woman's health in the second trimester and permitted states to prohibit abortion during the third trimester (when the fetus becomes viable), justifying this as fetal protection, as long as there was no risk to the life or health of the mother. The Court found that medical technology advancements had allowed for the viability of a fetus born at 23 or 24 weeks rather than at the 28-week point previously understood by the Court in *Roe*.

The legality of this practice was determined to be under the right to privacy and the First Amendment to the U.S. Constitution. The opposite conclusions were reached in this regard in *Tex. Med. Providers Performing Abortion Servs. v. Lakey*, 667 F.3d 570, 576 (5th Cir. 2012) and in *Stuart v. Huff*, 834 F. Supp. 2d 424 (M.D.N.C. 2011).

ABORTION LEGALITY IN THE U.S. TODAY

In 2022, the Supreme Court overturned *Roe v. Wade* and *Planned Parenthood v. Casey* in *Dobbs v. Jackson Women's Health Organization.*

***Dobbs v. Jackson Women's Health Organization*, No. 19-1392, 597 U.S.__ (2022)**

The court held that the Constitution of the United States does not confer a right to abortion. This decision reversed *Roe v. Wade* (1973) and *Planned Parenthood v. Casey*

(1992). Once again, as a result, the individual states were given the power to regulate all aspects of abortion not protected by federal law.

LEGISLATION IN THE VARIOUS STATES

Since the Supreme Court's decision in *Dobbs*, numerous states have enacted restrictions on abortion. Ultimately, it is expected that half of the states in the U.S. will impose restrictions on abortion following the Court's 2022 decision in *Dobbs*, which provided each state the right to regulate most aspects of abortion within their borders.

- Thirty-two states require that an abortion be performed only by a licensed physician. Twenty states require an abortion to be performed in a hospital after a specified point in the pregnancy, and seventeen states require the involvement of a second physician after a specified point.
- Forty-three states prohibit abortions after a specified point in pregnancy, with some exceptions provided. Most contentiously, a number of states, including Georgia and Texas, prohibit abortions (with specific exceptions) after what they term "fetal heartbeat," at six weeks into the pregnancy. The exceptions provided are generally when an abortion is necessary to protect the patient's life or health.
- Twenty-one states have laws in effect that prohibit "partial-birth" abortion. Three of these laws apply only to post-viability abortions.

Discussions of many states' new laws challenge these laws' requirements that the mother view an ultrasound and/or image, and/or hear the heartbeat of a fetus, before being allowed to abort.

THE NECESSITY DEFENSE IN CRIMINAL LAW

Many statutes regulate abortion. However, through the necessity defense, a woman may escape prosecution if the fetus threatens her life, even in jurisdictions where abortion is restricted.

Landmark cases from the 1800s, in which the defense of necessity was the plea of defendants charged with ending others' lives, later served as a precedent for legal arguments in cases pertaining to abortion. In these cases, individuals had been charged with a criminal act during an emergency, where they acted to prevent greater harm. In such circumstances, the U.S. legal system often excuses the individual's criminal act because it was justified or finds that no criminal act has occurred.

Several important requirements[6] limit the necessity defense:

- The defendant must reasonably have believed that an actual and specific threat required immediate action.
- The defendant must have had no realistic alternative to completing the criminal act.
- The harm caused by the criminal act must not be greater than the harm avoided.
- The defendant did not contribute to or cause the threat.

Only if all of these requirements are met will the defense of necessity be applicable. It is also important to note that in some jurisdictions, necessity is never permitted as a defense against killing another individual, no matter what threat this other individual may present.

Here are two of the landmark non-abortion-related cases that have addressed the necessity defense.

United States v. Holmes, 26 F. Cas. 360 (E.D. Pa. 1842)

This case addressed the question of whether self-defense is a valid plea for the charge of manslaughter.

In 1841, an American ship sank in the Atlantic Ocean. Nine crewmen and thirty-two passengers escaped the wreck in an overloaded longboat. Due to a storm, some of the

6. See Model Penal Code, §3.02.

crew, Alexander Holmes among them, forced twelve adult male passengers out of the longboat, in order that all forty-one aboard not perish. Later that day, the survivors were rescued by an American ship and taken to France.

After reaching their destination of Philadelphia, surviving passengers filed a complaint with the District Attorney, against the crew. The only crewman to be found was Holmes, so he alone was charged—with manslaughter. In *United States v. Holmes,* defense lawyers claimed that Holmes's actions were justified, as there was a necessity to save his own life.

While recognizing the concept that self-preservation is a defense to homicide, the judge instructed the jury that a seaman's duty is to protect the passengers, some of whom the crew had decided to sacrifice.

The jury "with some difficulty" found Holmes guilty. He was sentenced to six months in jail and a $20 fine (about $560 today).

Regina v. Dudley and Stephens, 14 Q.B.D. 273 (1884)

This case—concerning murder, as opposed to manslaughter as discussed above in *U.S. v. Holmes*—is a leading English criminal case that established a precedent throughout the common law world: that necessity is not a defense to a charge of murder.

Stranded on a lifeboat after their boat sunk in the Atlantic and after their food had run out, two sailors, Dudley and Stephens, killed a fellow sailor, Parker, to save themselves from dying from hunger.

The sailors were later rescued and brought to trial for murdering Parker. The defendants claimed the necessity defense. The Court found that there was no defense of necessity to a charge of murder, and thus the defendants were found to be guilty.

Dudley and Stephens were sentenced to the statutory death penalty with a recommendation for mercy. They were eventually released in 1885.

Lesson Four

SELECT U.S. LAW RELATED TO AUTOPSY AND ANATOMICAL DISSECTION

This lesson examines several principles relating to the use and handling of corpses when there is the intent of helping the still-living, including practices and laws concerning autopsy, grave-robbing, and other ways[7] of appropriating corpses for the purpose of medical training and research dissections.

DISSECTIONS AND AUTOPSY

Historically, dissections were generally forbidden by law. However, over the past three hundred years, exceptions have been made due to the demand for corpses for anatomical and medical research, most via legislation and some via court decisions.

The English Murder Act of 1751 (25 Geo. 2. c. 37) provided that "in no case whatsoever shall the body of any murderer be suffered to be buried" via mandating either "hanging in chains" of the cadaver following his execution or public dissection.

The (U.S.) Federal Crimes Act of 1790, §4, allowed a court to order the dissection of a corpse of a convicted and executed murderer. This provision of the statute was considered very controversial.

The Massachusetts Anatomy Act of 1831 permitted medical researchers to take possession of unclaimed bodies for science, thereby minimizing grave robberies.

In England, the Anatomy Act of 1832 provided access to unclaimed corpses, particularly those who had died in prisons or workhouses. It also stated that people could donate

7. May one steal or allow the bequest of a corpse to advance medical study and research or to save a terminal patient? The necessity defense—also explored in Lessons One and Three as applicable to "The Right to Try" and to abortion cases, respectively—might be a viable defense against criminal larceny charges in such a case.

Section 3.02 of the Model Penal Code allows for necessity as a defense to crimes when certain elements are met (See the bulleted list in Lesson Three, above). The official Commentary, which gives examples of situations where such a defense may work, states, "Mountain climbers lost in a storm may take refuge in a house or may appropriate provisions."

their next of kin's corpses to medical schools in exchange for post-dissection burial at the expense of the donee.

Enos v. Snyder, 131 Cal. 68 (1900)

In this case, a California Court held that existing law did not permit a man to bequeath his body before his death.

John Enos, who died in 1898, was survived by his wife, Susie Enos, and his mistress, Rachel Snyder; both women wanted control over his remains. Enos's will bequeathed his remains to Snyder. However, the court ruled that "there is no property in a dead body," that "it is not part of the estate of the deceased person, and that a man cannot by will dispose of that which after his death will be his corpse." Therefore, Mrs. Enos, as the decedent's closest relative, would retain custody of her husband's corpse because Mr. Enos had no right to will his corpse to Snyder. This ruling was followed by many other states as well.

The Uniform Anatomical Gift Act (UAGA)

The Uniform Anatomical Gift Act (UAGA) of 1968, along with its revisions in 1987 and 2006, has made body donation a legal right and established the human body as property. This privilege allowed a donor's wishes to be honored even if their next of kin objected to the donation after death.

The UAGA allows a decedent or surviving relatives to donate certain parts of the decedent's organs for specific purposes, such as giving to those in need or for medical research. Every state has enacted the provisions of the act in some form. The Act addresses the need for donations while respecting the religious and moral sensibilities of those who do not wish to donate.[8] Within four years, forty-eight states had adopted the UAGA, and today every state has adopted some form of the law.

8. Compare this to Maine's Anatomy Act of 1869: "If any resident of the state requests or consents that after his death his body may be delivered . . . for the advancement of anatomical science, it may be used for that purpose, unless some kindred or family connection makes objection."

The Religious Freedom Restoration Act (RFRA)

Lately, the state equivalents of the Religious Freedom Restoration Act (RFRA), a federal statute from 1993, have been enacted in many states, and courts in states that have not made laws protecting religious beliefs in autopsies found that the RFRA could prevent autopsies if the religion of the family of the deceased prohibited autopsies.

For example, a New York statute states that:

> In the absence of a compelling public necessity, no dissection or autopsy shall be performed over the objection of a surviving relative or friend of the deceased that such procedure is contrary to the religious belief of the decedent, or, if there is otherwise reason to believe that a dissection or autopsy is contrary to the decedent's religious beliefs. . . .
>
> "Compelling public necessity" shall mean: (i) that the dissection or autopsy is essential to the conduct of a criminal investigation of a homicide . . . of which the decedent is the victim, or (ii) that discovery of the cause of death is necessary to meet an immediate and substantial threat to the public health and that a dissection or autopsy is essential to ascertain the cause of death. . . .
>
> All dissections or autopsies performed pursuant to this section shall be the least intrusive procedure consistent with the compelling state interest.

See N.Y. PBH. Law § 4210-c: N.Y. Code - Section 4210-C: Limitations to Dissection or Autopsy. See also, *Johnson v. Levy*, No. M2009-02596 COA-R3-CV 2010 WL 119288 (Tenn. Ct. App. Jan. 14, 2010); and *Sanchez v. Saghian*, No. 01-07-00951-C, 2009 WL 3248266 (Tex. App.-Houston [1st Dist.] 2009).

Despite the shifts in biomedical ethics in the U.S. during the last three hundred years, there is still a shortage of donated cadavers. The shortage has led states to rely on their nineteenth-century laws allowing unclaimed bodies to be given to medical schools for dissection. Even though these laws were enacted well before society adopted autonomy as a central pillar of biomedical ethics, they have survived and carried over to today, leaving some to wonder whether this practice differs significantly from grave robbing.

Acknowledgments

We are grateful to the following individuals for their contributions to this course:

Flagship Director
RABBI SHMULY KARP

Curriculum Coordinator
RIVKI MOCKIN

Flagship Administrator
NAOMI HEBER

Author
RABBI SHMUEL SUPER

Editor
RABBI MORDECHAI DINERMAN

Course Consultant
RABBI EDWARD REICHMAN, M.D.

Curriculum Development Team
RABBI ELI RAKSIN
RABBI YANKY RASKIN
RABBI NAFTALI SILBERBERG
Medicine and Morals, Course Editor
MRS. CHANA SILBERSTEIN
Medicine and Morals, Course Author
RABBI YEHUDA PINK

Instructors Advisory Board
RABBI LEVI DUBOV
RABBI YOSSI MENDELSON
RABBI YOCHANAN POSNER
MRS. RIVKAH SLONIM

Legal Supplements
RABBI MENDY KATZMAN
MINDY WALLACH
YA'AKOVAH WEBER

Copywriters
RABBI YONI BROWN
RABBI YAAKOV PALEY

Proofreading
RACHEL MUSICANTE

Hebrew Punctuation
RABBI MOSHE WOLFF

Instructor Support
RABBI ISAAC ABELSKY
RABBI LEVI GOLDSHMID

Design and Layout Administrator
SARA OSDOBA

Textbook and Marketing Design
CHAYA MUSHKA KANNER
CHAYA KATZ
CHANA MARASOW
ESTIE RAVNOY
RABBI LEVI WEINGARTEN

Textbook Layout
RABBI MOTTI KLEIN

Imagery
SARA ROSENBLUM
CHAYA BARNETT
YA'AKOVAH WEBER

Permissions
SHULAMIS NADLER

Publication and Distribution
RABBI LEVI GOLDSHMID
RABBI MENDEL SIROTA

PowerPoint Presentations
SARA ROSENBLUM

Course Videos
GETZY RASKIN
MOSHE RASKIN

Key Points Videos
RABBI MOTTI KLEIN

We are immensely grateful for the encouragement of JLI's visionary chairman, and vice-chairman of *Merkos L'Inyonei Chinuch*—Lubavitch World Headquarters, **Rabbi Moshe Kotlarsky**. Rabbi Kotlarsky has been highly instrumental in building the infrastructure for the expansion of Chabad's international network and is also the architect of scores of initiatives and services to help Chabad representatives across the globe succeed in their mission. We are blessed to have the unwavering support of JLI's principal benefactor, **Mr. George Rohr**, who is fully invested in our work, continues to be instrumental in JLI's monumental growth and expansion, and is largely responsible for the Jewish renaissance that is being spearheaded by JLI and its affiliates across the globe.

The commitment and sage direction of JLI's dedicated Executive Board—**Rabbis Chaim Block**, **Hesh Epstein**, **Ronnie Fine**, **Yosef Gansburg**, **Shmuel Kaplan**, **Yisrael Rice**, and **Avrohom Sternberg**—and the countless hours they devote to the development of JLI are what drive the vision, growth, and tremendous success of the organization.

Finally, JLI represents an incredible partnership of more than 1,600 *shluchim* and *shluchot* in more than 1,000 locations across the globe, who contribute their time and talent to furthering Jewish adult education. We thank them for generously sharing feedback and making suggestions that steer JLI's development and growth. They are our most valuable critics and our most cherished contributors.

Inspired by the call of the **Lubavitcher Rebbe**, of righteous memory, it is the mandate of the Rohr JLI to provide a community of learning for all Jews throughout the world where they can participate in their precious heritage of Torah learning and experience its rewards. May this course succeed in fulfilling this sacred charge!

On behalf of the Rohr Jewish Learning Institute,

RABBI EFRAIM MINTZ
Executive Director

RABBI YISRAEL RICE
Chairman, Editorial Board

22 Shevat, 5784

The Rohr Jewish Learning Institute

CURRICULUM DEVELOPMENT

Rabbi Mordechai Dinerman
Rabbi Naftali Silberberg
EDITORS IN CHIEF

Rabbi Shmuel Klatzkin, PhD
ACADEMIC CONSULTANT

Rabbi Yanki Tauber
SENIOR EDITOR

Rabbi Eli Block
Rabbi Yoni Brown
Rabbi Eliezer Gurkow
Rabbi Meir Kerzner
Rabbi Berel Polityko
Rabbi Yochanan Rivkin
Rabbi Levi Shmotkin
Rabbi Shmuel Super
CURRICULUM AUTHORS

Rabbi Ahrele Loschak
EDITOR, TORAH STUDIES

Rabbi Yaakov Paley
WRITER

Rabbi Mendel Glazman
Mrs. Rochel Horowitz
Rabbi Moshe Wolff
EDITORIAL SUPPORT

Rabbi Yakov Gershon
RESEARCH

Rabbi Michoel Lipskier
Rabbi Mendel Rubin
EXPERIENTIAL LEARNING

Mrs. Rivki Mockin
CONTENT COORDINATOR

MARKETING AND BRANDING

Mr. David Kaplan
CHIEF MARKETING OFFICER

Ms. Miriam Posner
MARKETING ADMINISTRATOR

Yonatan Azrielant
Rabbi Mendel Backman
Risa Bursk
Baila Chemel
Lazer Cohen
Tova Farro
Yosef Feigelstock
Chana Wrubel
MARKETING AND SOCIAL MEDIA

Ms. Sara Osdoba
DESIGN ADMINISTRATOR

Mrs. Chaya Mushka Kanner
Mrs. Chaya Katz
Ms. Estie Ravnoy
Mrs. Shifra Tauber
Rabbi Levi Weingarten
GRAPHIC DESIGN

Rabbi Motti Klein
Rabbi Zalman Korf
Rabbi Moshe Wolff
PUBLICATION DESIGN

Rabbi Yaakov Paley
COPYWRITER

Rabbi Yossi Grossbaum
Rabbi Mendel Lifshitz
Rabbi Shraga Sherman
Rabbi Ari Sollish
Rabbi Mendel Teldon
MARKETING COMMITTEE

MARKETING CONSULTANTS

Alan Rosenspan
ALAN ROSENSPAN & ASSOCIATES
Sharon, MA

Gary Wexler
PASSION MARKETING
Los Angeles, CA

JLI CENTRAL

Rabbi Isaac Abelsky
Ms. Chanie Chesney
Rabbi Levi Goldshmid
Ms. Mushka Majeski
Ms. Mimi Rabinowitz
Rabbi Avremi Rapoport
Mrs. Aliza Scheinfeld
Ms. Mushka Silberstein
Rabbi Yosef Vogel
Rabbi Mendel Wolff
ADMINISTRATION

Ms. Liba Leah Gutnick
Rabbi Motti Klein
Mrs. Rochel Perlstein
Rabbi Shlomie Tenenbaum
PROJECT MANAGERS

Mrs. Mindy Wallach
AFFILIATE ORIENTATION

Ms. Chana Backman
Ms. Chaya Barnett
Ms. Tova Farro
Rabbi Motti Klein
Mrs. Chana Marasow
Getzy Raskin
Moshe Raskin
Mrs. Sara Rosenblum
MULTIMEDIA DEVELOPMENT

Rabbi Mendel Ashkenazi
Yoni Ben-Oni
Rabbi Mendy Elishevitz
Mendel Grossbaum
Mrs. Mushkie Osdoba
Rabbi Aron Liberow
Mrs. Chana Weinbaum
ONLINE DIVISION

Mrs. Rachel Musicante
Mrs. Ya'akovah Weber
PROOFREADERS

Rabbi Levi Goldshmid
Rabbi Mendel Sirota
PRINTING AND DISTRIBUTION

Mrs. Shaina B. Mintz
Mrs. Shulamis Nadler
Ms. Chinkah Zirkind
ACCOUNTING

Mrs. Chaya Katz
Mrs. Shulamis Nadler
Mrs. Mindy Wallach
CONTINUING EDUCATION

JLI FLAGSHIP

Rabbi Yisrael Rice
CHAIRMAN

Rabbi Shmuly Karp
DIRECTOR

Mrs. Naomi Heber
PROJECT MANAGER

PAST FLAGSHIP AUTHORS

Rabbi Yitzchak M. Kagan
of blessed memory

Rabbi Zalman Abraham
Brooklyn, NY

Rabbi Berel Bell
Montreal, QC

Rabbi Nissan D. Dubov
London, UK

Rabbi Tzvi Freeman
Atlanta, GA

Rabbi Eliezer Gurkow
London, ON

Rabbi Aaron Herman
Pittsburgh, PA

Rabbi Simon Jacobson
New York, NY

Rabbi Chaim D. Kagan, PhD
Monsey, NY

Rabbi Shmuel Klatzkin, PhD
Dayton, OH

Rabbi Nochum Mangel
Dayton, OH

Rabbi Moshe Miller, OBM
Chicago, IL

Rabbi Yosef Paltiel
Brooklyn, NY

Rabbi Yehuda Pink
Solihull, UK

Rabbi Yisrael Rice
S. Rafael, CA

Rabbi Eli Silberstein
Ithaca, NY

Mrs. Rivkah Slonim
Binghamton, NY

Rabbi Avrohom Sternberg
New London, CT

Rabbi Shais Taub
Cedarhurst, NY

Rabbi Shlomo Yaffe
Longmeadow, MA

ROSH CHODESH SOCIETY

Rabbi Shmuel Kaplan
CHAIRMAN

Mrs. Shaindy Jacobson
DIRECTOR

Mrs. Chana Dechter
ADMINISTRATOR

Mrs. Malky Bitton
Mrs. Shula Bryski
Mrs. Rochel Holzkenner
Mrs. Leah Rosenfeld
Mrs. Yehudis Wolvovsky
EDITORIAL BOARD

JLI TEENS

In Partnership with CTeen: Chabad Teen Network

Rabbi Chaim Block
CHAIRMAN

Rabbi Shlomie Tenenbaum
DIRECTOR

TORAH STUDIES

Rabbi Yosef Gansburg
CHAIRMAN

Rabbi Shlomie Tenenbaum
PROJECT MANAGER

Rabbi Ahrele Loschak
EDITOR

Rabbi Levi Fogelman
Rabbi Yaacov Halperin
Rabbi Nechemia Schusterman
Rabbi Ari Sollish
STEERING COMMITTEE

SINAI SCHOLARS SOCIETY

In Partnership with Chabad on Campus

Rabbi Menachem Schmidt
CHAIRMAN

Rabbi Dubi Rabinowitz
DIRECTOR

Ms. Miriam Spalter
PROJECT MANAGER

Ms. Yocheved Batya Michelashvili
Ms. Mussi Rabinowitz
Mrs. Manya Sperlin
COORDINATORS

Mrs. Devorah Zlatopolsky
ADMINISTRATOR

Rabbi Yossy Gordon
Rabbi Efraim Mintz
Rabbi Dubi Rabinowitz
Rabbi Menachem Schmidt
Mr. Thom Waye
Rabbi Avi Weinstein
EXECUTIVE COMMITTEE

Rabbi Chaim Leib Hilel
Rabbi Yossi Lazaroff
Rabbi Levi Raichik
Rabbi Shmuel Tiechtel
Rabbi Didy Waks
Rabbi Shmuly Weiss
STEERING COMMITTEE

THE WELLNESS INSTITUTE

Rabbi Zalman Abraham
VISION AND STRATEGIC PLANNING

Rabbi Menachem Klein
ADMINISTRATOR

Pamela Dubin
IMPACT ANALYSIS

Mindy Wallach
CONTINUING EDUCATION

Mushky Lipskier
EVENTS COORDINATOR

Dina Zarchi
ORGANIZATIONAL LIAISON

Moussie Lazaroff
Raizy Lifshitz
COMMUNICATIONS

Matti Feigelstock
PROJECT L'CHAIM COORDINATOR

Rivka Mogilevsky
TWI TORONTO COORDINATOR

Elisa Goldstein
TWI HOUSTON COORDINATOR

CLINICAL ADVISORY BOARD

Sigrid Frandsen-Pechenik, Psy.D.
CLINICAL DIRECTOR

Michele Borba, Ed.D.
David A. Brent, M.D.
Randal M. Erenst, Ed.D.
Gittel Francis, LMSW

Jill Harkavy-Friedman, PhD
Kenneth Ginsburg, M.D., M.S. Ed.
Madelyn S. Gould, PhD, MPH
Lisa A. Horowitz, PhD, MPH
Lisa Jacobs, M.D., MBA
Thomas Joiner, PhD
E. David Klonsky, PhD
Lisa Miller, PhD
Laura H. Mufson, PhD
Tayyab Rashid, PhD
Sylvia J. Sandler, LMFT
Bella Schanzer, M.D.
Andrew Shatté, PhD
Arielle H. Sheftall, PhD
Jonathan Singer, PhD, LCSW
Casey Skvorc, PhD, JD
Darcy Wallen, LCSW, PC

JLI INTERNATIONAL

Rabbi Avrohom Sternberg
CHAIRMAN

Rabbi Dubi Rabinowitz
DIRECTOR

Rabbi Mendel Glazman
ADMINISTRATOR

Rabbi Eli Wolf
ADMINISTRATOR, JLI IN THE CIS

In Partnership with the Federation of Jewish Communities of the CIS

Flor Setton
COORDINATOR,
CHABAD OF ARGENTINA

Rabbi Nochum Schapiro
REGIONAL REPRESENTATIVE, AUSTRALIA

Rabbi Avrohom Steinmetz
REGIONAL REPRESENTATIVE, BRAZIL

Rabbi Shevach Zlatopolsky
EDITOR, JLI IN THE CIS

Rabbi Shlomo Cohen
FRENCH COORDINATOR,
REGIONAL REPRESENTATIVE

Rabbi Avraham Golovacheov
REGIONAL REPRESENTATIVE, GERMANY

Rabbi Shlomo Koves
REGIONAL REPRESENTATIVE, HUNGARY

Rabbi Shmuel Katzman
REGIONAL REPRESENTATIVE,
NETHERLANDS

Rabbi Bentzi Sudak
REGIONAL REPRESENTATIVE,
UNITED KINGDOM

NATIONAL JEWISH RETREAT

Rabbi Hesh Epstein
CHAIRMAN

Mrs. Shaina B. Mintz
DIRECTOR

Bruce Backman
HOTEL LIAISON

Rabbi Menachem Klein
PROGRAM COORDINATOR

Rabbi Isaac Mintz
SHLUCHIM LIAISON

Rabbi Mendel Rosenfeld
LOGISTICS COORDINATOR

Ms. Mushka Majeski
Mrs. Aliza Scheinfeld
SERVICE AND SUPPORT

THE LAND & THE SPIRIT
Israel Experience

Rabbi Shmuly Karp
DIRECTOR

Rabbi Isaac Mintz
SHLUCHIM LIAISON

Mrs. Shaina B. Mintz
ADMINISTRATOR

Rabbi Yechiel Baitelman
Rabbi Dovid Flinkenstein
Rabbi Chanoch Kaplan
Rabbi Levi Klein
Rabbi Mendy Mangel
Rabbi Sholom Raichik
STEERING COMMITTEE

SHABBAT IN THE HEIGHTS

Rabbi Shmuly Karp
DIRECTOR

Mrs. Shulamis Nadler
SERVICE AND SUPPORT

Rabbi Chaim Hanoka
CHAIRMAN

Rabbi Mordechai Dinerman
Rabbi Zalman Marcus
STEERING COMMITTEE

MYSHIUR
Advanced Learning Initiative

Rabbi Shmuel Kaplan
CHAIRMAN

Rabbi Shlomie Tenenbaum
ADMINISTRATOR

TORAHCAFE.COM
Online Learning

Rabbi Mendy Elishevitz
WEBSITE DEVELOPMENT

Moshe Levin
CONTENT MANAGER

Mendel Laine
FILMING

MACHON SHMUEL
The Sami Rohr Research Institute

Rabbi Zalman Korf
ADMINISTRATOR

Rabbi Moshe Miller, OBM
Rabbi Gedalya Oberlander
Rabbi Chaim Rapoport
Rabbi Levi Yitzchak Raskin
Rabbi Chaim Schapiro
RABBINIC ADVISORY BOARD

Rabbi Yakov Gershon
RESEARCH FELLOW

FOUNDING DEPARTMENT HEADS

Rabbi Mendel Bell
Rabbi Zalman Charytan
Rabbi Mendel Druk
Rabbi Menachem Gansburg
Rabbi Meir Hecht
Rabbi Levi Kaplan
Rabbi Yoni Katz
Rabbi Chaim Zalman Levy
Rabbi Benny Rapoport
Dr. Chana Silberstein
Rabbi Elchonon Tenenbaum
Rabbi Mendy Weg

JLI Chapter Directory

ALABAMA

BIRMINGHAM
Rabbi Yossi Friedman 205.970.0100

MOBILE
Rabbi Yosef Goldwasser 251.265.1213

ALASKA

ANCHORAGE
Rabbi Yosef Greenberg
Rabbi Mendy Greenberg 907.357.8770

ARIZONA

CHANDLER
Rabbi Mendy Deitsch 480.855.4333

FLAGSTAFF
Rabbi Dovie Shapiro 928.255.5756

FOUNTAIN HILLS
Rabbi Mendy Lipskier 480.776.4763

ORO VALLEY
Rabbi Ephraim Zimmerman 520.477.8672

PARADISE VALLEY
Rabbi Shlomo Levertov 480.788.9310

PHOENIX
Rabbi Dovber Dechter 347.410.0785
Rabbi Zalman Levertov
Rabbi Yossi Friedman 602.944.2753

PRESCOTT
Rabbi Elie Filler 928.362.8924

SCOTTSDALE
Rabbi Yossi Levertov 480.998.1410

SEDONA
Rabbi Mendel Kessler 928.985.0667

TUCSON
Rabbi Yehuda Ceitlin 520.881.7956

VAIL
Rabbi Yisroel Shemtov 347.372.3092

ARKANSAS

LITTLE ROCK
Rabbi Pinchus Ciment 501.217.0053

CALIFORNIA

AGOURA HILLS
Rabbi Moshe Bryski 818.516.0444

ALAMEDA
Rabbi Meir Shmotkin 510.640.2590

ARCADIA
Rabbi Sholom Stiefel 626.539.4578

BAKERSFIELD
Rabbi Shmuli Schlanger 661.834.1512

BEL AIR
Rabbi Chaim Mentz 310.475.5311

BEL AIR WEST
Rabbi Mendy Mentz 310.666.2302

BEVERLY HILLS
Rabbi Dovid Begun 310.242.7750

BEVERLYWOOD
Rabbi Menachem Mendel Piekarski 310.597.0967

BURBANK
Rabbi Shmuly Kornfeld 818.954.0070

CARLSBAD
Rabbi Yeruchem Eilfort
Mrs. Nechama Eilfort 760.943.8891

CERRITOS
Rabbi Mendel Lehrer 917.717.8704

CHATSWORTH
Rabbi Yossi Spritzer 818.307.9907

CHULA VISTA
Rabbi Mendy Begun 347.587.0979

CONCORD
Rabbi Berel Kesselman 925.326.1613

CONTRA COSTA
Rabbi Dovber Berkowitz 925.937.4101

CORONADO

Rabbi Eli Fradkin 619.365.4728

DANA POINT

Rabbi Eli Goorevitch 949.290.0628

DANVILLE

Rabbi Shmuli Raitman 213.447.6694

EMERYVILLE

Rabbi Menachem Blank 510.859.8808

ENCINO

Rabbi Aryeh Herzog 818.784.9986

Chapter founded by Rabbi Joshua Gordon, OBM

FOLSOM

Rabbi Yossi Grossbaum 916.608.9811

FREMONT

Rabbi Eli Landes 510.300.4090

GLENDALE

Rabbi Simcha Backman 818.240.2750

HIGHLAND PARK

Rabbi Mendel Korf 323.872.4876

HOLLYWOOD

Rabbi Zalman Partouche 818.964.9428

HUNTINGTON BEACH

Rabbi Aron David Berkowitz 714.846.2285

IRVINE

Rabbi Elly Andrusier 949.786.5000

LAGUNA NIGUEL

Rabbi Mendy Paltiel 949.831.7701

LA JOLLA

Rabbi Baruch Shalom Ezagui 858.455.5433

LAKE BALBOA

Rabbi Eli Gurary 347.403.6734

LOMITA

Rabbi Sholom Pinson 310.326.8234

LONG BEACH

Rabbi Abba Perelmuter 562.773.1350

LOS ANGELES

Rabbi Yossi Elifort 310.515.5310
Rabbi Leibel Korf 323.660.5177
Rabbi Zalmy Labkowsky 213.618.9486
Rabbi Mendel Zajac 310.770.9051

MALIBU

Rabbi Levi Cunin 310.456.6588

MAR VISTA

Rabbi Shimon Simpson 646.401.2354

MARINA DEL REY

Rabbi Danny Yiftach-Hashem
Rabbi Dovid Yiftach 310.859.0770

MILL VALLEY

Rabbi Hillel Scop 415.336.3055

NEWHALL

Rabbi Choni Marosov 661.254.3434

NEWPORT BEACH

Rabbi Reuven Mintz 949.375.3707

NORTHRIDGE

Rabbi Eli Rivkin 818.368.3937

OJAI

Rabbi Mordechai Nemtzov 805.613.7181

PACIFIC PALISADES

Rabbi Zushe Cunin 310.454.7783

PALO ALTO

Rabbi Menachem Landa 415.418.4768
Rabbi Yosef Levin
Rabbi Ber Rosenblatt 650.424.9800

PASADENA

Rabbi Zushe Rivkin 626.788.3343

PLEASANTON

Rabbi Josh Zebberman 925.846.0700

PORTOLA VALLEY

Rabbi Mayer Brook 650.304.2098

POWAY

Rabbi Mendel Goldstein 858.208.6613

RANCHO CUCAMONGA

Rabbi Sholom Ber Harlig 909.949.4553

RANCHO MIRAGE
Rabbi Shimon H. Posner 760.770.7785

RANCHO PALOS VERDES
Rabbi Yitzchok Magalnic 310.544.5544

RANCHO S. FE
Rabbi Levi Raskin 858.756.7571

REDONDO BEACH
Rabbi Yossi Mintz
Rabbi Zalman Gordon 310.214.4999

RESEDA
Rabbi Hershy Spritzer 818.881.1033

RIVERSIDE
Rabbi Shmuel Fuss 951.329.2747

S. CLEMENTE
Rabbi Menachem M. Slavin 949.489.0723

S. CRUZ
Rabbi Yochanan Friedman 831.454.0101

S. DIEGO
Rabbi Rafi Andrusier 619.387.8770
Rabbi Yechiel Cagen 832.216.1534
Rabbi Motte Fradkin 858.547.0076

S. FRANCISCO
Rabbi Yakov Barber 424.499.9868
Rebbetzin Mattie Pil 415.933.4310
Rabbi Gedalia Potash 415.648.8000
Rabbi Shlomo Zarchi 415.752.2866

S. LUIS OBISPO
Rabbi Meir Gordon 347.675.3383

S. MATEO
Rabbi Yossi Marcus 650.341.4510

S. RAFAEL
Rabbi Yisrael Rice 415.492.1666

SHERMAN OAKS
Rabbi Nachman Abend 818.989.9539

SONOMA
Rabbi Mendel Wolvovsky 707.292.6221

SOUTH LAKE TAHOE
Rabbi Mordechai Richler 530.539.4363

SOUTH PASADENA
Rabbi Dovid Harlig 626.921.6256

STOCKHOLM
Rabbi Avremel Brod 209.952.2081

SUNNYVALE
Rabbi Yisroel Hecht 408.720.0553

TEMECULA
Rabbi Yonason Abrams 951.234.4196

TIBURON
Rabbi Levi Mintz 415.378.9364

TOPANGA
Rabbi Menachem Piekarski 858.335.7197

TUSTIN
Rabbi Yehoshua Eliezrie 714.508.2150

VACAVILLE
Rabbi Chaim Zaklos 707.592.5300

WEST HILLS
Rabbi Avi Rabin 818.337.4544

WEST HOLLYWOOD
Rabbi Mordechai Kirschenbaum 310.691.9988

WEST LOS ANGELES
Rabbi Mordechai Zaetz 424.652.8742

WOODLAND HILLS
Rabbi Menachem Mendel Gordon 818.917.8456

YORBA LINDA
Rabbi Dovid Eliezrie 714.693.0770

COLORADO

ASPEN
Rabbi Mendel Mintz 970.544.3770

DENVER
Rabbi Mendel Popack 720.515.4337
Rabbi Yossi Serebryanski 303.744.9699
Rabbi Mendy Sirota 720.940.3716

FORT COLLINS
Rabbi Yerachmiel Gorelik 970.407.1613

HIGHLANDS RANCH
Rabbi Avraham Mintz 303.694.9119

LONGMONT
Rabbi Yakov Borenstein 303.678.7595

VAIL
Rabbi Dovid Mintz 970.476.7887

WESTMINSTER
Rabbi Benjy Brackman 303.429.5177

CONNECTICUT

FAIRFIELD
Rabbi Shlame Landa 203.373.7551

GLASTONBURY
Rabbi Yosef Wolvovsky 860.659.2422

GREENWICH
Rabbi Yossi Deren
Rabbi Menachem Feldman 203.629.9059

GUILFORD
Rabbi Yossi Yaffe 203.645.4635

HAMDEN
Rabbi Moshe Hecht 203.635.7268

MILFORD
Rabbi Schneur Wilhelm 203.887.7603

NEW HAVEN
Rabbi Mendy Hecht 203.589.5375
Rabbi Chanoch Wineberg 203.479.0313

NEW LONDON
Rabbi Avrohom Sternberg 860.437.8000

ORANGE
Rabbi Hershy Hecht 203.464.7809

SHELTON
Rabbi Schneur Brook 203.364.4149

STAMFORD
Rabbi Yisrael Deren
Rabbi Levi Mendelow 203.3.CHABAD

WEST HARTFORD
Rabbi Shaya Gopin 860.232.1116

WESTPORT
Rabbi Yehuda Kantor 561.460.3758

DELAWARE

WILMINGTON
Rabbi Chuni Vogel 302.529.9900

DISTRICT OF COLUMBIA
Rabbi Levi Shemtov
Rabbi Yitzy Ceitlin 202.332.5600

FLORIDA

ALTAMONTE SPRINGS
Rabbi Mendy Bronstein 407.280.0535

AVENTURA
Rabbi Mendel Rosenblum 412.807.0584

BOCA RATON
Rabbi Zalman Bukiet 561.487.2934
Rabbi Moishe Denburg 561.526.5760
Rabbi Arele Gopin 561.994.6257
Rabbi Ruvi New 561.394.9770

BONITA SPRINGS
Rabbi Mendy Greenberg 239.949.6900

BOYNTON BEACH
Rabbi Sholom Ciment 561.732.4633
Rabbi Yosef Yitzchok Raichik 561.740.8738

BRADENTON
Rabbi Menachem Bukiet 941.388.9656

CAPE CORAL
Rabbi Yossi Labkowski 239.963.4770

CORAL GABLES
Rabbi Avrohom Stolik 305.490.7572

CORAL SPRINGS
Rabbi Hershy Bronstein 954.798.6023
Rabbi Yankie Denburg 954.471.8646

CUTLER BAY
Rabbi Yossi Wolff 305.975.6680

DAVIE
Rabbi Aryeh Schwartz 954.376.9973

DELRAY BEACH
Rabbi Yaakov Perman 561.666.2770

FISHER ISLAND
Rabbi Efraim Brody 347.325.1913

FLEMING ISLAND
Rabbi Shmuly Feldman 904.290.1017

FORT LAUDERDALE
Rabbi Schneur Kaplan 954.667.8000
Rabbi Yitzchok Naparstek 954.568.1190

HALLANDALE BEACH
Rabbi Mordy Feiner 954.458.1877

HOLLYWOOD
Rabbi Leibel Kudan 954.801.3367

JUPITER
Rabbi Berel Barash 561.317.0968

KENDALL
Rabbi Yossi Harlig 305.234.5654

KEY BISCAYNE
Rabbi Avremel Caroline 305.365.6744

LAUDERHILL
Rabbi Shmuel Heidingsfeld 323.877.7703

LONGWOOD
Rabbi Yanky Majesky 407.636.5994

MAITLAND
Rabbi Sholom Dubov
Rabbi Levik Dubov 470.644.2500
Rabbi Tzviki Dubov 407.529.8256

MARION COUNTY
Rabbi Yossi Hecht 352.330.4466

MIAMI
Rabbi Mendy Cheruty 305.219.3353
Rabbi Yakov Fellig 305.445.5444
Rabbi Shmuel Gopin 305.573.9995
Rabbi Chaim Lipskar 305.373.8303

MIAMI BEACH
Rabbi Yisroel Frankforter 305.534.3895
Rabbi Sholom Korf 786.423.6483
Rabbi Shmuel Mann 305.674.8400

N. MIAMI BEACH
Rabbi Eli Laufer 305.770.4412

NAPLES
Rabbi Fishel Zaklos 239.404.6993

ORLANDO
Rabbi Yosef Konikov 407.354.3660

ORMOND BEACH
Rabbi Asher Farkash 386.672.9300

PALM BEACH
Rabbi Zalman Levitin 561.659.3884

PALM BEACH GARDENS
Rabbi Dovid Vigler 561.624.2223

PALM CITY
Rabbi Shlomo Uminer 772.485.5501

PALM HARBOR
Rabbi Pinchas Adler 727.789.0408

PARKLAND
Rabbi Mendy Gutnick 954.600.6991

PEMBROKE PINES
Rabbi Mordechai Andrusier 954.874.2280

PENSACOLA
Rabbi Mendel Danow 850.291.9600

PLANTATION
Rabbi Pinchas Taylor 954.644.9177

PONTE VEDRA BEACH
Rabbi Nochum Kurinsky 904.543.9301

PORT ORANGE
Rabbi Mendel Niasoff 386.679.5756

ROYAL PALM BEACH
Rabbi Nachmen Zeev Schtroks 561.714.1692

S. AUGUSTINE
Rabbi Levi Vogel 904.521.8664

S. JOHNS
Rabbi Mendel Sharfstein 347.461.3765

S. PETERSBURG
Rabbi Alter Korf 727.344.4900

SARASOTA
Rabbi Chaim Shaul Steinmetz 941.925.0770
Rabbi Levi Steinmetz 941.928.9267

SATELLITE BEACH

Rabbi Zvi Konikov 321.777.2770

SINGER ISLAND

Rabbi Berel Namdar 347.276.6985

SOUTH PALM BEACH

Rabbi Leibel Stolik 561.889.3499

SOUTH TAMPA

Rabbi Mendy Dubrowski 813.922.1723

SOUTHWEST BROWARD COUNTY

Rabbi Aryeh Schwartz 954.252.1770

SUNNY ISLES BEACH

Rabbi Alexander Kaller 305.803.5315

SURFSIDE

Rabbi Dov Schochet 305.790.8294

TAMARAC

Rabbi Kopel Silberberg 954.882.7434

TAMPA

Rabbi Chaim Lipszyc 954.882.7434

VENICE

Rabbi Sholom Ber Schmerling 845.238.0770

VERO BEACH

Rabbi Motty Rosenfeld 772.245.6712

WATERWAYS

Rabbi Yisroel Brusowankin 786.663.8731

WESLEY CHAPEL

Rabbi Mendy Yarmush

Rabbi Mendel Friedman 813.731.2977

WEST DELRAY BEACH

Rabbi Yossi Schapiro 561.221.1618

WEST PALM BEACH

Rabbi Yoel Gancz 561.659.7770

WESTON

Rabbi Yisroel Spalter 954.349.6565

GEORGIA

ALPHARETTA

Rabbi Hirshy Minkowicz 770.410.9000

ATLANTA

Rabbi Yossi New

Rabbi Isser New 404.843.2464

Rabbi Alexander Piekarski 678.267.6418

Rabbi Ari Sollish 404.898.0434

ATLANTA: INTOWN

Rabbi Eliyahu Schusterman

Rabbi Chanan Rose 415.370.1333

AUGUSTA

Rabbi Zalman Fischer 706.836.1576

CUMMING

Rabbi Levi Mentz 310.666.2218

DUNWOODY

Rabbi Mendy Wineberg 347.770.2414

GAINESVILLE

Rabbi Nechemia Gurevitz 770.906.4970

GWINNETT

Rabbi Yossi Lerman 678.595.0196

MARIETTA

Rabbi Ephraim Silverman 770.565.4412

HAWAII

KAILUA-KONA

Rabbi Levi Gerlitzky 917.853.2787

KAPA'A

Rabbi Michoel Goldman 808.647.4293

IDAHO

BOISE

Rabbi Mendel Lifshitz 208.853.9200

ILLINOIS

ARLINGTON HEIGHTS

Rabbi Yaakov Kotlarsky 224.357.7002

CHAMPAIGN

Rabbi Dovid Tiechtel 217.355.8672

CHICAGO

Rabbi Mendy Benhiyoun 312.498.7704
Rabbi Mordechai Gershon 773.412.5189
Rabbi Dovid Kotlarsky 773.495.7127
Rabbi Yosef Moscowitz 773.772.3770
Rabbi Levi Notik 773.274.5123

ELGIN

Rabbi Mendel Shemtov 847.440.4486

GLENVIEW

Rabbi Yishaya Benjaminson 847.910.1738

GURNEE

Rabbi Sholom Tenenbaum 847.782.1800

HIGHLAND PARK

Mrs. Michla Schanowitz 847.266.0770

NAPERVILLE

Rabbi Mendy Goldstein 630.957.8122

NORTHBROOK

Rabbi Meir Moscowitz 847.564.8770

NORWOOD PARK

Rabbi Mendel Perlstein 312.752.8894

OAK PARK

Rabbi Yitzchok Bergstein 708.524.1530

PARK RIDGE

Rabbi Lazer Hershkovich 224.392.4442

PEORIA

Rabbi Eli Langsam 309.370.7701

SKOKIE

Rabbi Yochanan Posner 847.677.1770

VERNON HILLS

Rabbi Shimmy Susskind 718.755.5356

WILMETTE

Rabbi Dovid Flinkenstein 847.251.7707

INDIANA

INDIANAPOLIS

Rabbi Avraham Grossbaum
Rabbi Dr. Shmuel Klatzkin 317.251.5573

IOWA

BETTENDORF

Rabbi Shneur Cadaner 563.355.1065

KANSAS

OVERLAND PARK

Rabbi Mendy Wineberg 913.649.4852

KENTUCKY

LOUISVILLE

Rabbi Avrohom Litvin 502.459.1770

LOUISIANA

BATON ROUGE

Rabbi Peretz Kazen 225.267.7047

METAIRIE

Rabbi Yossie Nemes
Rabbi Mendel Ceitlin 504.454.2910

NEW ORLEANS

Rabbi Mendel Rivkin 504.302.1830

MAINE

BANGOR

Rabbi Chaim Wilansky 207.650.7223

PORTLAND

Rabbi Levi Wilansky 207.650.1783

MARYLAND

BALTIMORE

Rabbi Velvel Belinsky 410.764.5000
Classes in Russian

Rabbi Dovid Reyder 781.796.4204

BEL AIR

Rabbi Kushi Schusterman 443.353.9718

BETHESDA

Rabbi Sender Geisinsky 301.913.9777

CHEVY CHASE

Rabbi Zalman Minkowitz 301.260.5000

COLUMBIA

Rabbi Hillel Baron

Rabbi Yosef Chaim Sufrin 410.740.2424

FREDERICK

Rabbi Boruch Labkowski 301.996.3659

GAITHERSBURG

Rabbi Sholom Raichik 301.926.3632

OLNEY

Rabbi Bentzy Stolik 301.660.6770

OWINGS MILLS

Rabbi Nochum Katsenelenbogen 410.356.5156

POTOMAC

Rabbi Mendel Bluming 301.983.4200

Rabbi Mendel Kaplan 301.983.1485

ROCKVILLE

Rabbi Shlomo Beitsh 646.773.2675

Rabbi Moishe Kavka 301.836.1242

MASSACHUSETTS

ANDOVER

Rabbi Asher Bronstein 978.470.2288

ARLINGTON

Rabbi Avi Bukiet 617.909.8653

BOSTON

Rabbi Yosef Zaklos 617.297.7282

BRIGHTON

Rabbi Dan Rodkin 617.787.2200

CAPE COD

Rabbi Yekusiel Alperowitz 508.775.2324

CHESTNUT HILL

Rabbi Mendy Uminer 617.738.9770

LEXINGTON

Rabbi Yisroel New 646.248.9053

LONGMEADOW

Rabbi Yakov Wolff 413.567.8665

NEWTON

Rabbi Shalom Ber Prus 617.244.1200

PEABODY

Rabbi Nechemia Schusterman 978.977.9111

SUDBURY

Rabbi Yisroel Freeman 978.443.0110

SWAMPSCOTT

Rabbi Yossi Lipsker 781.581.3833

VINEYARD HAVEN

Rabbi Tzvi Alperowitz 508.560.8650

MICHIGAN

ANN ARBOR

Rabbi Aharon Goldstein 734.995.3276

BLOOMFIELD HILLS

Rabbi Levi Dubov 248.949.6210

GRAND RAPIDS

Rabbi Mordechai Haller 616.957.0770

TROY

Rabbi Menachem Caytak 248.873.5851

WEST BLOOMFIELD

Rabbi Zelig Shemtov 248.788.4000

Rabbi Elimelech Silberberg 248.855.6170

MINNESOTA

MINNETONKA

Rabbi Mordechai Grossbaum

Rabbi Shmuel Silberstein 952.929.9922

PLYMOUTH

Rabbi Nissan Naparstek 310.430.0960

S. PAUL

Rabbi Shneur Zalman Bendet 651.998.9298

MISSOURI

CHESTERFIELD

Rabbi Avi Rubenfeld 314.258.3401

S. LOUIS

Rabbi Yosef Abenson 314.448.0927

Rabbi Yosef Landa 314.725.0400

MONTANA

BOZEMAN
Rabbi Chaim Shaul Bruk 406.600.4934

KALISPELL
Rabbi Shneur Wolf 406.885.2541

NEVADA

LAS VEGAS
Rabbi Yosef Rivkin 702.217.2170

RENO
Rabbi Levi Sputz 347.262.4531

SUMMERLIN
Rabbi Yisroel Schanowitz
Rabbi Tzvi Bronchtain 702.855.0770

NEW JERSEY

BASKING RIDGE
Rabbi Mendy Herson
Rabbi Mendel Shemtov 908.604.8844

CHERRY HILL
Rabbi Mendel Mangel 856.874.1500

CLINTON
Rabbi Eli Kornfeld 908.623.7000

ENGLEWOOD
Rabbi Shmuel Konikov 201.519.7343

FAIR LAWN
Rabbi Avrohom Bergstein 201.794.3770

FANWOOD
Rabbi Avrohom Blesofsky 908.790.0008

FLANDERS
Rabbi Yaacov Shusterman 973.723.6868

FORT LEE
Rabbi Meir Konikov 201.886.1238

GREATER MERCER COUNTY
Rabbi Dovid Dubov
Rabbi Yaakov Chaiton 609.213.4136

HASKELL
Rabbi Mendy Gurkov 201.696.7609

HOLMDEL
Rabbi Shmaya Galperin 732.772.1998

JACKSON
Rabbi Shmuel Naparstek 732.668.7702

JERICHO
Rabbi Mendy Brownstein 516.850.4486

MADISON
Rabbi Shalom Lubin 973.377.0707

MANALAPAN
Rabbi Boruch Chazanow
Rabbi Levi Wolosow 732.972.3687

MEDFORD
Rabbi Yitzchok Kahan 609.451.3522

MONTCLAIR
Rabbi Yaacov Leaf 862.252.5666

MORRISTOWN
Rabbi Moishe Gurevitz 973.216.8077

MOUNTAIN LAKES
Rabbi Levi Dubinsky 973.551.1898

MULLICA HILL
Rabbi Avrohom Richler 856.733.0770

OLD TAPPAN
Rabbi Mendy Lewis 201.767.4008

RANDOLPH
Rabbi Avraham Bekhor 718.915.8748

RED BANK
Rabbi Dovid Harrison 973.895.3070

ROCKAWAY
Rabbi Asher Herson
Rabbi Mordechai Baumgarten 973.625.1525

RUTHERFORD
Rabbi Yitzchok Lerman 347.834.7500

SCOTCH PLAINS
Rabbi Avrohom Blesofsky 908.790.0008

SHORT HILLS
Rabbi Mendel Solomon
Rabbi Avrohom Levin 973.725.7008

SOUTH BRUNSWICK
Rabbi Levi Azimov 732.398.9492

TENAFLY
Rabbi Mordechai Shain 201.871.1152

TOMS RIVER
Rabbi Moshe Gourarie 732.349.4199

VENTNOR
Rabbi Avrohom Rapoport 609.822.8500

WEST ORANGE
Rabbi Mendy Kasowitz 973.325.6311

WOODCLIFF LAKE
Rabbi Dov Drizin 201.476.0157

NEW MEXICO

LAS CRUCES
Rabbi Bery Schmukler 575.524.1330

NEW YORK

ALBANY
Rabbi Mordechai Rubin 518.368.7886

BEDFORD
Rabbi Arik Wolf 914.666.6065

BENSONHURST
Rabbi Avrohom Hertz 718.753.7768

BINGHAMTON
Mrs. Rivkah Slonim 607.797.0015

BRIGHTON BEACH
Rabbi Dovid Okonov 718.368.4490

BRONXVILLE
Rabbi Sruli Deitsch 917.755.0078

BROOKVILLE
Rabbi Mendy Heber 516.626.0600

CEDARHURST
Rabbi Zalman Wolowik 516.295.2478

CLIFTON PARK
Rabbi Yossi Rubin 518.495.0772

COMMACK
Rabbi Mendel Teldon 631.543.3343

DELMAR
Rabbi Zalman Simon 518.866.7658

DOBBS FERRY
Rabbi Benjy Silverman 914.693.6100

EAST HAMPTON
Rabbi Leibel Baumgarten
Rabbi Mendy Goldberg 631.329.5800

ELLENVILLE
Rabbi Shlomie Deren 845.647.4450

FOREST HILLS
Rabbi Yossi Mendelson 917.861.9726

GLEN OAKS
Rabbi Shmuel Nadler 347.388.7064

GREAT NECK
Rabbi Yoseph Geisinsky 516.487.4554

ISLIP
Rabbi Shimon Stillerman 631.913.8770

KINGSTON
Rabbi Yitzchok Hecht 845.334.9044

LARCHMONT
Rabbi Mendel Silberstein 914.834.4321

LITTLE NECK
Rabbi Eli Shifrin 718.423.1235

LONG BEACH
Rabbi Eli Goodman 516.574.3905

LONG ISLAND CITY
Rabbi Zev Wineberg 347.218.2927

MANHASSET
Rabbi Mendel Paltiel 516.984.0701

MELVILLE
Rabbi Yosef Raskin 631.276.4453

MINEOLA
Rabbi Anchelle Perl 516.739.3636

MONTEBELLO
Rabbi Shmuel Gancz 845.746.1927

NEW HARTFORD
Rabbi Levi Charitonow 716.322.8692

NEW YORK
Rabbi Yakov Bankhalter 917.613.1678
Rabbi Nissi Eber 347.677.2276
Rabbi Berel Gurevitch 212.518.3122
Rabbi Daniel Kraus 917.294.5567
Rabbi Shmuel Metzger 212.758.3770

NYC TRIBECA
Rabbi Zalman Paris 212.566.6764

NYC UPPER EAST SIDE
Rabbi Uriel Vigler 212.369.7310

NYC WEST SIDE
Rabbi Shlomo Kugel 212.864.5010

OCEANSIDE
Rabbi Levi Gurkow 516.764.7385

OSSINING
Rabbi Dovid Labkowski 914.923.2522

OYSTER BAY
Rabbi Shmuel Lipszyc
Rabbi Shalom Lipszyc 347.853.9992

PARK SLOPE
Rabbi Menashe Wolf 347.957.1291

PORT WASHINGTON
Rabbi Shalom Paltiel 516.767.8672

PROSPECT HEIGHTS
Rabbi Mendy Hecht 347.622.3599

ROCHESTER
Rabbi Nechemia Vogel 585.271.0330

ROSLYN
Rabbi Yaakov Reiter 516.484.3500

ROSLYN HEIGHTS
Rabbi Aaron Konikov 516.484.3500

SEA GATE
Rabbi Chaim Brikman 347.524.3214

SOUTHAMPTON
Rabbi Chaim Pape 917.627.4865

STATEN ISLAND
Rabbi Mendy Katzman 718.370.8953

STONY BROOK
Rabbi Shalom Ber Cohen 631.585.0521

SUFFERN
Rabbi Shmuel Gancz 845.368.1889

WEST BRIGHTON BEACH
Rabbi Moshe Winner 718.946.9833

YORKTOWN HEIGHTS
Rabbi Yehuda Heber 914.962.1111

NORTH CAROLINA

CARY
Rabbi Yisroel Cotlar 919.651.9710

CHAPEL HILL
Rabbi Zalman Bluming 919.357.5904

CHARLOTTE
Rabbi Yossi Groner
Rabbi Shlomo Cohen 704.366.3984

GREENSBORO
Rabbi Yosef Plotkin 336.617.8120

RALEIGH
Rabbi Pinchas Herman
Rabbi Mendy Wilschanski 919.847.8986

WILMINGTON
Rabbi Moshe Lieblich 910.763.4770

WINSTON-SALEM
Rabbi Levi Gurevitz 336.756.9069

OHIO

BEACHWOOD
Rabbi Moshe Gancz 216.647.4884

CINCINNATI
Rabbi Yisroel Mangel 513.793.5200

COLUMBUS
Rabbi Yitzi Kaltmann 614.294.3296

DAYTON
Rabbi Nochum Mangel 937.643.0770

OKLAHOMA

OKLAHOMA CITY
Rabbi Ovadia Goldman 405.524.4800

TULSA
Rabbi Yehuda Weg 918.492.4499

OREGON

PORTLAND
Rabbi Mordechai Wilhelm 503.977.9947

SALEM
Rabbi Avrohom Yitzchok Perlstein 503.383.9569

TIGARD
Rabbi Menachem Orenstein 971.329.6661

WEST LINN
Rabbi Shimon Wilhelm 503.753.4744

PENNSYLVANIA

AMBLER
Rabbi Shaya Deitsch 215.591.9310

BALA CYNWYD
Rabbi Shraga Sherman 610.660.9192

CLARKS SUMMIT
Rabbi Benny Rapoport 570.587.3300

DOYLESTOWN
Rabbi Mendel Prus 215.340.1303

FREEDOM
Rabbi Yosef Feller 612.275.6438

GLEN MILLS
Rabbi Yehuda Gerber 484.620.4162

LAFAYETTE HILL
Rabbi Yisroel Kotlarsky 484.533.7009

LANCASTER
Rabbi Elazar Green 717.723.8783

LEWISBURG
Rabbi Yisroel Baumgarten 631.880.2801

MECHANICSBURG
Rabbi Nissen Pewzner 717.798.0053

MONROEVILLE
Rabbi Mendy Schapiro 412.372.1000

NEWTOWN
Rabbi Aryeh Weinstein 215.497.9925

PHILADELPHIA
Rabbi Berel Paltiel 718.288.8574

PHILADELPHIA: CENTER CITY
Rabbi Yochonon Goldman 215.238.2100

PITTSBURGH
Rabbi Yisroel Altein .... 412.422.7300 EXT. 269

PITTSBURGH: SOUTH HILLS
Rabbi Mendy Rosenblum 412.278.3693

READING
Rabbi Yosef Lipsker 610.334.3218

RYDAL
Rabbi Zushe Gurevitz 267.536.5757

UNIVERSITY PARK
Rabbi Nosson Meretsky 814.863.4929

WYNNEWOOD
Rabbi Moishe Brennan 610.529.9011

PUERTO RICO

CAROLINA
Rabbi Mendel Zarchi 787.253.0894

RHODE ISLAND

WARWICK
Rabbi Yossi Laufer 101.881.7888

SOUTH CAROLINA

BLUFFTON
Rabbi Menachem Hertz 843.301.1819

COLUMBIA
Rabbi Hesh Epstein
Rabbi Levi Marrus 803.782.1831

GREENVILLE
Rabbi Leibel Kesselman 864.534.7739

MYRTLE BEACH
Rabbi Doron Aizenman 843.448.0035

TENNESSEE

CHATTANOOGA
Rabbi Shaul Perlstein 423.910.9770

KNOXVILLE
Rabbi Yossi Wilhelm 865.588.8584

MEMPHIS
Rabbi Levi Klein 901.754.0404

NASHVILLE
Rabbi Yitzchok Tiechtel 615.646.5750

TEXAS

AUSTIN
Rabbi Mendy Levertov 512.905.2778

BELLAIRE
Rabbi Yossi Zaklikofsky 713.839.8887

CYPRESS
Rabbi Levi Marinovsky 832.651.6964

DALLAS
Rabbi Zvi Drizin 214.632.2633
Rabbi Mendel Dubrawsky
Rabbi Moshe Naparstek 972.818.0770

EL PASO
Rabbi Levi Greenberg 347.678.9762

FORT WORTH
Rabbi Dov Mandel 817.263.7701

HOUSTON
Rabbi Dovid Goldstein
Rabbi Zally Lazarus 281.589.7188
Rabbi Moishe Traxler 713.774.0300

HOUSTON: RICE UNIVERSITY AREA
Rabbi Eliezer Lazaroff 713.522.2004

LEAGUE CITY
Rabbi Yitzchok Schmukler 281.724.1554

PLANO
Rabbi Eli Block 214.620.4083
Rabbi Mendel Block 972.596.8270

ROCKWALL
Rabbi Moshe Kalmenson 469.350.5735

ROUND ROCK
Rabbi Mendel Marasow 512.387.3171

S. ANTONIO
Rabbi Chaim Block
Rabbi Levi Teldon 210.492.1085
Rabbi Tal Shaul 210.877.4218

SOUTHLAKE
Rabbi Levi Gurevitch 817.451.1171

SUGAR LAND
Rabbi Mendel Feigenson 832.758.0685

THE WOODLANDS
Rabbi Mendel Blecher 281.865.7242

UTAH

LEHI
Rabbi Chaim Zippel 801.674.4566

PARK CITY
Rabbi Yehuda Steiger 435.714.8590

S. GEORGE
Rabbi Mendy Cohen 862.812.6224

SALT LAKE CITY
Rabbi Benny Zippel 801.467.7777

VERMONT

BURLINGTON
Rabbi Yitzchok Raskin 802.658.5770

MANCHESTER
Rabbi Menachem Andrusier 518.506.8678

WATERBURY CENTER
Rabbi Boruch Simon 518.360.7337

VIRGINIA

ALEXANDRIA/ARLINGTON
Rabbi Mordechai Newman 703.370.2774

FAIRFAX
Rabbi Leibel Fajnland 703.426.1980

GAINESVILLE
Rabbi Shmuel Perlstein 571.445.0342

LOUDOUN COUNTY
Rabbi Chaim Cohen 248.298.9279

NORFOLK
Rabbi Aaron Margolin
Rabbi Levi Brashevitzky 757.616.0770

RICHMOND
Rabbi Shlomo Pereira 804.740.2000

WINCHESTER
Rabbi Yishai Dinerman 540.324.9879

WASHINGTON

BAINBRIDGE ISLAND
Rabbi Mendy Goldshmid 206.397.7679

BELLINGHAM
Rabbi Yosef Truxton 360.224.9919

KIRKLAND
Rabbi Chaim S. Rivkin 425.749.8512

LYNNWOOD
Rabbi Berel Paltiel 425.286.7465

MERCER ISLAND
Rabbi Elazar Bogomilsky 206.527.1411
Rabbi Nissan Kornfeld 206.851.2324

NORMANDY PARK
Rabbi Moshe Wolff 206.946.2477

OLYMPIA
Rabbi Yosef Schtroks 360.867.8804

SEATTLE
Rabbi Yoni Levitin 206.851.9831
Rabbi Shmuel Levitin 347.415.2271
Rabbi Shnai Levitin 347.342.2259

SPOKANE COUNTY
Rabbi Yisroel Hahn 509.443.0770

WISCONSIN

BAYSIDE
Rabbi Cheski Edelman 414.439.5041

BROOKFIELD
Rabbi Levi Brook 925.708.4203

KENOSHA
Rabbi Tzali Wilschanski 262.359.0770

MADISON
Rabbi Avremel Matusof 608.335.3777

MEQUON
Rabbi Menachem Rapoport 262.242.2235

MILWAUKEE
Rabbi Levi Emmer 414.277.8839
Rabbi Mendel Shmotkin 414.961.6100

WYOMING

LARAMIE
Rabbi Yaakov Raskin 307.920.2613

ARGENTINA

BAHIA BLANCA
Rabbi Shmuel Freedman 347.300.2779

BUENOS AIRES
Rabbi Abraham Benchimol 54.11.6048.5333
Rabbi Yossi Birman 54.11.5334.6606
Mrs. Chani Gorowitz 54.11.4865.0445
Rabbi Menachem M. Grunblatt 54.911.3574.0037
Rabbi Mendy Gurevitch 55.11.4545.7771
Rabbi Mendel Levy 54.11.3687.8258
Rabbi Shlomo Levy 54.11.4807.2223
Rabbi Yosef Levy 54.11.4504.1908
Rabbi Yosef Yitzjok Levy 54.11.0292.4125
Rabbi Tzvi Lipinsky 54.11.5249.2693
Rabbi Yossi Ludman 54.11.3935.0214
Rabbi Yoel Migdal 54.11.4963.1221
Rabbi Mendi Mizrahi 54.11.4963.1221
Rabbi Shiele Plotka 54.11.4634.3111
Rabbi Itzjak Safranchik 54.11.3699.3977
Rabbi Shniur Zalmen Schvetz 54.11.3552.5208
Rabbi Shloimi Setton 54.11.4982.8637
Rabbi Pinhas Sudry 54.1.4822.2285

CORDOBA
Rabbi Menajem Turk 54.351.233.8250

ROSARIO
Rabbi Shlomo Tawil 54.93.4152.0039

S. MIGUEL DE TUCUMÁN

Rabbi Ariel Levy 54.381.473.6944

SALTA

Rabbi Rafael Tawil 54.387.421.4947

AUSTRALIA

NEW SOUTH WALES

BELLEVUE HILL

Mrs. Chaya Kaye 614.3342.2755

DOUBLE BAY

Rabbi Yanky Berger 612.9327.1644

DOVER HEIGHTS

Rabbi Motti Feldman 614.0400.8572

MAROUBRA

Rabbi Schneur Goldstein 614.3476.0722

NEWTOWN

Rabbi Eli Feldman 614.0077.0613

NORTH SHORE

Rabbi Nochum Schapiro
Rebbetzin Fruma Schapiro 612.9488.9548

SYDNEY

Rabbi Levi Wolff 614.2162.2622

THE HILL

Rabbi Yossi Rodal 614.2573.0412

QUEENSLAND

BOKARINA

Rabbi Asher Goodman 898.6763.0334

BRISBANE

Rabbi Levi Jaffe 617.3843.6770

TASMANIA

SOUTH LAUNCESTON

Mrs. Rochel Gordon 614.2055.0405

VICTORIA

EAST S. KILDA

Rabbi Sholem Gorelik 614.5244.8770

MOORABBIN

Rabbi Elisha Greenbaum 614.0349.0434

WESTERN AUSTRALIA

PERTH

Rabbi Shalom White 618.9275.2106

AZERBAIJAN

BAKU

Mrs. Chavi Segal 994.12.597.91.90

BELARUS

BOBRUISK

Mrs. Mina Hababo 375.29.104.3230

MINSK

Rabbi Shneur Deitsch
Mrs. Bassie Deitsch 375.29.330.6675

BELGIUM

ANTWERP

Rabbi Mendel Gurary 32.48.656.9878

BRUSSELS

Rabbi Shmuel Pinson 375.29.330.6675

BRAZIL

CURITIBA

Rabbi Mendy Labkowski 55.41.3079.1338

S. PAULO

Rabbi Avraham Steinmetz 55.11.3081.3081

CANADA

ALBERTA

CALGARY

Rabbi Mordechai Groner 403.281.3770

EDMONTON

Rabbi Ari Drelich
Rabbi Mendy Blachman 780.200.5770

BRITISH COLUMBIA

COQUITLAM

Rabbi Benzti Shemtov 250.797.7877

NANAIMO

Rabbi Mordechai Gurevitz 604.787.5667

RICHMOND

Rabbi Yechiel Baitelman 604.277.6427

VANCOUVER

Rabbi Dovid Rosenfeld 604.266.1313

Rabbi Shmuel Yeshayahu 604.738.7060

VICTORIA

Rabbi Meir Kaplan 250.595.7656

MANITOBA

WINNIPEG

Rabbi Shmuel Altein 204.339.8737

ONTARIO

BAYVIEW

Rabbi Levi Gansburg 416.551.9391

EAST THORNHILL

Rabbi Mendel Zaltzman 647.998.7105

GREATER TORONTO REGIONAL OFFICE & THORNHILL

Rabbi Yossi Gansburg 905.731.7000

KINGSTON

Rabbi Yisroel Simon 613.770.1884

MAPLE

Rabbi Yechezkel Deren 647.883.6372

MISSISSAUGA

Rabbi Yitzchok Slavin 905.820.4432

NORTH YORK

Rabbi Sruli Steiner 647.501.5618

OTTAWA

Rabbi Menachem M. Blum 613.843.7770

Rabbi Moshe Caytak 613.902.4394

RICHMOND HILL

Rabbi Mendel Bernstein 905.303.1880

TORONTO

Rabbi Sholom Lezell 416.809.1365

Rabbi Shmuel Neft 647.966.7105

Rabbi Moshe Steiner 416.635.9606

WATERLOO

Rabbi Moshe Goldman 226.338.7770

WHITBY

Rabbi Tzali Borenstein 905.447.8215

QUEBEC

CÔTE S.-LUC

Rabbi Levi Naparstek 438.409.6770

DOLLARD-DES ORMEAUX

Rabbi Leibel Fine 514.777.4675

HAMPSTEAD

Rabbi Moshe New

Rabbi Berel Bell 514.739.0770

MONTREAL

Rabbi Ronnie Fine

Pesach Nussbaum 514.738.3434

MONTREAL WEST

Rabbi Mendy Marlow 514.632.9649

OLD MONTREAL/GRIFFINTOWN

Rabbi Nissan Gansbourg

Rabbi Berel Bell 514.800.6966

S. LAURENT

Rabbi Schneur Zalmen Silberstein 514.747.1199

S. LAZARE

Rabbi Nochum Labkowski 514.436.7426

TOWN OF MOUNT ROYAL

Rabbi Moshe Krasnanski

Rabbi Shneur Zalman Rader 514.342.1770

SASKATCHEWAN

SASKATOON

Rabbi Raphael Kats 306.384.4370

CAYMAN ISLANDS

GEORGE TOWN

Rabbi Berel Pewzner 717.798.1040

COLOMBIA

BOGOTA

Rabbi Chanoch Piekarski 57.1.635.8251

COSTA RICA

S. JOSÉ

Rabbi Hershel Spalter

Rabbi Moshe Bitton 506.4010.1515

CROATIA

ZAGREB

Rabbi Pinchas Zaklas 385.1.481.2227

DENMARK

COPENHAGEN

Rabbi Yitzchok Loewenthal 45.3316.1850

DOMINICAN REPUBLIC

S. DOMINGO

Rabbi Shimon Pelman 829.341.2770

ESTONIA

TALLINN

Rabbi Shmuel Kot 372.662.30.50

FRANCE

BOULOGNE

Rabbi Michael Sojcher 33.1.46.99.87.85

DIJON

Rabbi Chaim Slonim 33.6.52.05.26.65

LA VARENNE-S.-HILAIRE

Rabbi Mena'hem Mendel Benelbaz 33.6.17.81.57.47

MARSEILLE

Rabbi Eliahou Altabe 33.6.11.60.03.05

Rabbi Mena'hem Mendel Assouline 33.6.64.88.25.04

Rabbi Emmanuel Taubenblatt 33.4.88.00.94.85

PARIS

Rabbi Yona Hasky 33.1.53.75.36.01

Rabbi Acher Marciano 33.6.15.15.01.02

Rabbi Avraham Barou'h Pevzner 33.6.99.64.07.70

PONTAULT-COMBAULT

Rabbi Yossi Amar 33.6.61.36.07.70

VILLIERS-SUR-MARNE

Rabbi Mena'hem Mendel Mergui 33.1.49.30.89.66

GEORGIA

TBILISI

Rabbi Meir Kozlovsky 995.32.2429770

GERMANY

BERLIN

Rabbi Yehuda Tiechtel 49.30.2128.0830

DUSSELDORF

Rabbi Chaim Barkahn 49.173.2871.770

HAMBURG

Rabbi Shlomo Bistritzky 49.40.4142.4190

HANNOVER 49.511.811.2822

Chapter founded by Rabbi Binyamin Wolff, OBM

GREECE

ATHENS

Rabbi Mendel Hendel 30.210.323.3825

GUATEMALA

GUATEMALA CITY

Rabbi Shalom Pelman 502.2485.0770

HUNGARY

BUDAPEST

Rabbi Shlomo Kovesh 361.268.0183

IRELAND

DUBLIN

Rabbi Zalman Lent 3538.7419.5354

ISRAEL

ASHKELON

Rabbi Shneor Lieberman 054.977.0512

BALFURYA

Rabbi Noam Bar-Tov 054.580.4770

CAESAREA

Rabbi Chaim Meir Lieberman 054.621.2586

EVEN YEHUDA

Rabbi Menachem Noyman 054.777.0707

GANEI TIKVA

Rabbi Gershon Shnur 054.524.2358

GIV'ATAYIM

Rabbi Pinchus Bitton 052.643.8770

JERUSALEM

Rabbi Levi Diamond 055.665.7702
Rabbi Avraham Hendel 054.830.5799

KARMIEL

Rabbi Mendy Elishevitz 054.521.3073

KFAR SABA

Rabbi Yossi Baitch 054.445.5020

KIRYAT BIALIK

Rabbi Pinny Marton 050.661.1768

KIRYAT MOTZKIN

Rabbi Shimon Eizenbach 050.902.0770

KOCHAV YAIR

Rabbi Dovi Greenberg 054.332.6244

MACCABIM-RE'UT

Rabbi Yosef Yitzchak Noiman 054.977.0549

NESS ZIONA

Rabbi Menachem Feldman 054.497.7092

NETANYA

Rabbi Schneur Brod 054.579.7572

RAMAT GAN-KRINITZI

Rabbi Yisroel Gurevitz 052.743.2814

RAMAT GAN-MAROM NAVE

Rabbi Binyamin Meir Kali 050.476.0770

RAMAT YISHAI

Rabbi Shneor Zalman Wolosow 052.324.5475

RISHON LEZION

Rabbi Uri Keshet 050.722.4593

ROSH PINA

Rabbi Sholom Ber Hertzel 052.458.7600

TEL AVIV

Rabbi Shneur Piekarski 054.971.5568

JAMAICA

MONTEGO BAY

Rabbi Yaakov Raskin 876.452.3223

JAPAN

TOKYO

Rabbi Mendi Sudakevich 81.3.5789.2846

KAZAKHSTAN

ALMATY

Rabbi Shevach Zlatopolsky 7.7272.77.59.49

KYRGYZSTAN

BISHKEK

Rabbi Arye Raichman 996.312.68.19.66

LATVIA

RIGA

Rabbi Shneur Zalman Kot
Mrs. Rivka Glazman 371.6720.40.22

LITHUANIA

VILNIUS

Rabbi Sholom Ber Krinsky 370.6817.1367

LUXEMBOURG

LUXEMBOURG

Rabbi Mendel Edelman 352.2877.7079

MEXICO

PUERTO VALLARTA

Rabbi Shneur Hecht 52.32.2141.7279

S. MIGUEL DE ALLENDE

Rabbi Daniel Huebner 52.41.5181.8092

NETHERLANDS

ALMERE

Rabbi Moshe Stiefel 31.36.744.0509

AMSTERDAM

Rabbi Yanki Jacobs 31.644.988.627
Rabbi Jaacov Zwi Spiero 31.652.328.065

EINDHOVEN

Rabbi Simcha Steinberg 31.63.635.7593

HAGUE

Rabbi Shmuel Katzman 31.70.347.0222

HEEMSTEDE-HAARLEM

Rabbi Shmuel Spiero 31.23.532.0707

MAASTRICHT

Rabbi Avrohom Cohen 32.48.549.6766

NIJMEGEN

Rabbi Menachem Mendel Levine 31.621.586.575

ROTTERDAM

Rabbi Yehuda Vorst 31.10.265.5530

PANAMA

PANAMA CITY

Rabbi Ari Laine

Rabbi Gabriel Benayon 507.223.3383

RUSSIA

ASTRAKHAN

Rabbi Yisroel Melamed 7.851.239.28.24

BRYANSK

Rabbi Menachem Mendel Zaklas 7.483.264.55.15

CHELYABINSK

Rabbi Meir Kirsh 7.351.263.24.68

MOSCOW

Rabbi Aizik Rosenfeld 7.906.762.88.81

Rabbi Mordechai Weisberg 7.495.645.50.00

NIZHNY NOVGOROD

Rabbi Shimon Bergman 7.920.253.47.70

NOVOSIBIRSK

Rabbi Shneur Zalmen Zaklos 7.903.900.43.22

OMSK

Rabbi Osher Krichevsky 7.381.231.33.07

PERM

Rabbi Zalman Deutch 7.342.212.47.32

ROSTOV

Rabbi Chaim Danzinger 7.8632.99.02.68

S. PETERSBURG

Rabbi Shalom Pewzner 7.911.726.21.19

Rabbi Zvi Pinsky 7.812.713.62.09

SAMARA

Rabbi Shlomo Deutch 7.846.333.40.64

SARATOV

Rabbi Yaakov Kubitshek 7.8452.21.58.00

TOGLIATTI

Rabbi Meier Fischer 7.848.273.02.84

UFA

Rabbi Dan Krichevsky 7.347.244.55.33

VORONEZH

Rabbi Levi Stiefel 7.473.252.96.99

SINGAPORE

SINGAPORE

Rabbi Mordechai Abergel 656.337.2189

Rabbi Netanel Rivni 656.336.2127

Classes in Hebrew

SOUTH AFRICA

JOHANNESBURG

Rabbi Dovid Masinter

Rabbi Ari Kievman 27.11.440.6600

SWEDEN

STOCKHOLM

Rabbi Chaim Greisman 46.70.790.8994

SWITZERLAND

LUZERN

Rabbi Chaim Drukman 41.41.361.1770

THAILAND

BANGKOK

Rabbi Yosef C. Kantor 6681.837.7618

UKRAINE

BERDITCHEV

Mrs. Chana Thaler 380.637.70.37.70

DNEPROPETROVSK

Rabbi Dan Makagon 380.504.51.13.18

NIKOLAYEV

Rabbi Sholom Gotlieb 380.512.37.37.71

ODESSA

Rabbi Avraham Wolf

Rabbi Yaakov Neiman .... 38.048.728.0770 EXT. 280

ZAPOROZHYE

Mrs. Nechama Dina Ehrentreu 380.957.19.96.08

ZHITOMIR

Rabbi Shlomo Wilhelm 380.504.63.01.32

UNITED KINGDOM

BOURNEMOUTH

Rabbi Bentzion Alperowitz 44.749.456.7177

CHEADLE

Rabbi Peretz Chein 44.161.428.1818

ESSEX

EPPING

Rabbi Yossi Posen 44.749.650.4345

LEEDS

Rabbi Eli Pink 44.113.266.3311

LONDON

Rabbi Moshe Adler 44.771.052.4460
Rabbi Boruch Altein 44.749.612.3342
Rabbi Mendel Cohen 44.736.640.8244
Rabbi Mechel Gancz 44.758.332.3074
Rabbi Chaim Hoch 44.753.879.9524
Rabbi Mendel Kalmanson 44.758.592.0195
Rabbi Dovid Katz 44.207.625.2682
Mrs. Esther Kesselman 44.794.432.4829
Rabbi Mendy Korer 44.794.632.5444
Rabbi Baruch Levin 44.208.905.4141
Rabbi Eli Levin 44.754.046.1568
Mrs. Chanie Simon 44.208.458.0416
Rabbi Bentzi Sudak 44.781.211.1890
Rabbi Yisroel Weisz 44.797.652.2807
Rabbi Shneur Wineberg 44.716.628.6538

MANCHESTER

Rabbi Levi Cohen 44.161.792.6335
Rabbi Shmuli Jaffe 44.161.766.1812

NOTTINGHAM

Rabbi Mendy Lent 44.759.005.1261

RADLETT, HERTFORDSHIRE

Rabbi Alexander Sender Dubrawsky 44.794.380.8965

Notes

Notes

Notes

Notes

Notes

Notes

Notes

Notes

The Jewish Learning Multiplex

Brought to you by the Rohr Jewish Learning Institute

In fulfillment of the mandate of the Lubavitcher Rebbe, of blessed memory, whose leadership guides every step of our work, the mission of the Rohr Jewish Learning Institute is to transform Jewish life and the greater community through the study of Torah, connecting each Jew to our shared heritage of Jewish learning.

While our flagship program remains the cornerstone of our organization, JLI is proud to feature additional divisions catering to specific populations, in order to meet a wide array of educational needs.

THE ROHR JEWISH LEARNING INSTITUTE

A subsidiary of Merkos L'Inyonei Chinuch,
the adult education arm of the Chabad-Lubavitch movement

Torah Studies provides a rich and nuanced encounter with the weekly Torah reading.

Jewish teens forge their identity as they engage in Torah study, social interaction, and serious fun.

The Rosh Chodesh Society gathers Jewish women together once a month for intensive textual study.

TorahCafe.com provides an exclusive selection of top-rated Jewish educational videos.

Participants delve into our nation's past while exploring the Holy Land's relevance and meaning today.

This yearly event rejuvenates mind, body, and spirit with a powerful synthesis of Jewish learning and community.

Equips youths facing adulthood with education and resources to address youth mental health

Select affiliates are invited to partner with peers and noted professionals, as leaders of innovation and excellence.

MyShiur courses are designed to assist students in developing the skills needed to study Talmud independently.

This rigorous fellowship program invites select college students to explore the fundamentals of Judaism.

A crash course that teaches adults to read Hebrew in just five sessions

Machon Shmuel is an institute providing Torah research in the service of educators worldwide.